I Need a Better Friend

Authored by
Mel Ann Sullivan

Edited by
Sarah Elizabeth Odom, Ph.D.
Janet Wallace

Cover Design and Photography by
Lorie Roach Photography
Daisy Breanna Sullivan

Published July 2016

II Chron 16:9

Table of Contents

About the Author		3
Introduction		4
Chapter 1	The Promise of the Past	7
Chapter 2	The Reality of the Present	16
Chapter 3	The Purpose of the Future	27
Chapter 4	Befriend Who?	43
Chapter 5	Sojourners in Friendship	60
Chapter 6	Abraham, Friend of God	79
Chapter 7	Moses, Face to Face	90
Chapter 8	Servant, Friend of God	106
Chapter 9	You, Friend of God	126

About the Author

No sooner had the Lord given Mel Ann Sullivan Psalm 37:4 as a promise than she began to see the people she loved most taken from her. Her mother was diagnosed with brain cancer just weeks before Mel Ann graduated from high school, and lost the battle after 14 months. Four years later, her father had a fatal automobile accident. She and her husband had just celebrated their first anniversary. By anyone's standards, it would not be the best way to enter adult life.

After 29 years of marriage and three children, God has given Mel Ann the desires of her heart, and not the least of them - the delight of a relationship with Christ that far exceeds salvation alone.

Saved at a young age, Mel Ann began a journey to now call Christ "Savior," and bow to Him as "Lord." In the absence of the strongest support they'd ever known, the losses brought a stark awakening to Mel Ann and her siblings as they depended on the Lord in a new way.

Mel Ann and Gary live in Millry, Alabama. Their children are young adults, and are pursuing their degrees. They are serving members of Calvary Baptist Church in Waynesboro, Mississippi, and enjoy simple rural living. She holds a B.A. from the School of Communication at the University of Alabama, and loves writing and speaking, both in Christian service and professionally. She is employed with a community bank in Alabama as a marketing/communications director, and is also the bank's community development officer.

Introduction

True friends are hard to find. If you can count your closest friends on just a few fingers, you should consider yourself blessed indeed. This book is about friendship – being a friend, having a friend. Few thoughts are sweeter than knowing someone is your friend. I saw a recent quote that sums up the value of friendships worth finding, "Friendship isn't about who you've known the longest. It's about who walked into your life and said, 'I'm here for you' and proved it." – Author Unknown

This is my first book, and I am not sure exactly how I got to the end of it. But I know how it began. When God speaks, we can't see Him. Very few have had the opportunity to audibly hear His voice. But when He speaks in His own way, I am finally listening! The Lord's gentle whisper was clear to me - not audible, but clear. "Write a book on friendship." The subject matter was all too familiar. The week before, I had composed some notes in preparation for a speaking engagement. The Lord illuminated John 21 a year earlier calling me to be His friend. But write a book? Wait a minute, Lord? I'll need some strong confirmation. Many books are available by excellent, experienced authors and scholars. Why? It'll probably never be published. Who'll care? I had many questions, like these: Was that you, Lord? Did you say what I think you said?

I'm grateful He didn't grow weary from all my questions. Interrogation might be a better word to describe it. I was willing to obey, but I asked Him to confirm what He had told me. So in the same sitting, I had already prepared a brief testimony I was asked to share at my church. After I did, our pastor delivered the day's message: "No Excuses". My heart pounded and burned as He preached from the book of Jonah - the one who ran from

God's call. He ran as far and as deep as he could before he finally obeyed.

The one who runs from God is a miserable soul. I'm sure Jonah was miserably sick in the belly of that fish. Jonah did not immediately obey because: 1) He misunderstood the challenge; and 2) He misunderstood the urgency. Our pastor urged us to trade fear for faith, noting that fear often stands as the arch-enemy of obedience in a walk of faith. When we fail to obey, we misunderstand the challenge and urgency of God's plan.

The arrow of God's plan went straight from His heart to mine. I started writing, and was compelled to continue until the work was complete. After 12 rounds of edits, and a last round by my editor, Sarah Elizabeth Odom, Ph.D., it's a work that God started inside of me and has allowed me the privilege to complete. I invite you to journey with me and learn what it means to befriend the God of all creation through His Son. He has been the ultimate Friend of mankind for generations, but He also calls you to be His friend. You might ask, like I have – "But Lord, how can I be your friend? You have been my Friend. You have rescued me, ministered to me, and comforted me for as long as I can remember. How can you possibly want *me* as your friend? Lord, you need Billy Graham, D.L. Moody, or others of great faith and stature, but *me?*"

Abraham was called *my friend* by God Himself. The Lord spoke with Moses face to face as a man would speak to his friend. In John 21, Peter was called to friendship with the Lord Jesus. We, His disciples and servants, are also called to befriend Christ. What is it about these men that God endeared them as friends?

Take this journey with me, won't you? Join me to learn who this faithful Friend is as He speaks to you through scripture. It is a privilege to serve you from the table of God's Word. I will feast as you feast, and learn as you are learning. Traveling with friends is always fulfilling, so thanks for joining me. We've got quite a journey.

1
The Promise of the Past

     We begin with an eye on Peter's early days as a disciple, his sifting, the denial and return to service. As we peer into his life, we'll run a background check on this fisherman from Christ's catch to see not only the pit from which he was called, but also his purpose. A promising future, he was the "little rock" on which the first church was built. He was passionate, yet impulsive; a leader, yet still learning to follow; and full of life, yet fearful of death. Common among those who have come any distance with Christ, Peter also had a past. On the road God was leading this disciple, it was a past that He would use. Putting our "before" behind us is not always possible. It's never good to forget the state of life from which God has redeemed us.

     You've got a story to tell, and it includes your before *and* your after. We'll find Peter transformed when this story winds down. Here's a brief profile of Peter from the Life Application Bible (NIV):

- He and his brother, Andrew, were the first disciples to be called (Matt. 4:18-22).
- Peter, James and John were the only three invited to the transfiguration of Christ on the mountain (Mark 9:2).
- He became the recognized leader among the disciples.
- Peter was the first great voice of the Gospel during and after Pentecost.
- Peter's story is told in the Gospels and Acts.
- He wrote 1 and 2 Peter.

     Though we won't study his life in-depth, we'll look at Peter from certain angles. The view we'll take is the time of his sifting, and ultimately his denial of knowing

Christ. It's a privilege to study God's Word with you as we peer into Peter's life and other friends of God.

A Purposeful Pondering

"And I tell you that you are Peter, and on this rock I will build my church, and the gates of Hades will not overcome it. Matt. 16:18 NIV

Let's look at some ponderings Peter had to consider. Christ had reason for the questions He asked. He still asks them today, and we are wise to ponder their answers for the purpose of life lies in them.

When you read Matthew 16:13-18, you'll notice a smattering of questions. Questions can be annoying, can't they? Our unrelenting children repeat the same questions to get our attention. Often times, I'll ask my husband something that deserves an answer. He'll respond with a question. When the Lord questions, there is always a reason. Why do you believe Jesus first asked, "Who do people say that I am?"

We can only speculate. He already knew how they perceived Him and what their answers would be. Peter reminds me of the young student who raises his hand repeatedly to answer questions. Manners and class rules are thrown out in the competitive clatter to be the first student with the right response. One of those times for him is in Matt. 16:15-18. Any of them could have answered. But Peter blurted out what he knew to be true. He not only knew Christ, he identified Christ as the Son of the living God.

In verse 18, we see two rocks. The New Strong's Exhaustive Concordance of the Bible defines the name Peter as *petros* meaning a fragment of a bigger rock. In the same verse, the word rock is *petra*, meaning boulder or cliff. The Lord knew Peter before he was born (Is. 44:2).

He gave him this new name, "a piece of the rock", long before he would have the character to match it. Peter would be a church planter, a rock of strength for the early church.

Who do you say Jesus is? The Father in Heaven reveals it to you, so thank Him now if you responded as Peter did. Do you have difficulty answering this question? Pray now and ask the Father to reveal His Son to you. Ask a Christian friend, family member or pastor to pray with and encourage you in your search for faith in Christ.
Has the Lord revealed to you His purposes for this time of your life? *What on earth am I here for?* is the subtitle of a popular book that has now sold more than 30 million copies. Sales soar because it's something we all search to find: our purpose in life. We are to walk in daily obedience before God. Waiting for something big to happen is the worst enemy to living out God's plan. Maybe, like me (and Peter), you have cast out many times to reel in the biggest and best catch. You may have thought, *so this is what life is all about.* Peter discovered what life was all about, and so can we when we cross paths with Christ.

Crossing Paths

I want you to know, brothers, that the gospel I preach is not something that man made up. Galatians 1:11 NIV

Peter met the person of Christ. Their places in time overlapped for that very reason. Though Paul did not cross paths with Christ in the flesh, he did bow to the call and message of the cross. And He met up with some interesting characters after his conversion.

Paul crossed paths with Jesus' disciples in his first years of ministry. He may have been anxious to meet Jesus' first disciples. Though I might have placed them on pedestals, Paul makes sure we know his revelation did not come through them. In the passage above, what does Paul say about how he *did not* receive the Gospel?

Paul followed by faith the Christ that the disciples first followed with their feet. Three years into his journey with Christ, Paul crossed paths with Peter for a 15-day stay. Why do you think he stayed with Peter 15 days? Do you know another Christian to whom you are drawn? If so, what is it about that person that attracts you to him or her?

When it was time to part ways, perhaps they both left strengthened and encouraged, ready to continue ministering in the name of the Lord. In Galatians 2:8, Paul compares their ministries and God's work. "For God, who was at work in the ministry of Peter as an apostle to the Jews, was also at work in my ministry as an apostle to the Gentiles." They had the same call, but different paths to cross, and diverse circles of influence.

Something else took place to benefit Paul in his ministry after being with Peter, James, and John (see Gal. 2:9). They gave him Barnabas when they recognized the grace he had received from God. The Lord mightily used Peter *and* Paul. Though their callings had been made known, Paul persecuted Christ before his calling, and Peter would deny Christ after his. God's grace makes them useful for His glory either way. Our usefulness is wrapped up in Christ. He alone says, "Come, follow me." Perhaps today, your circle of influence includes those sweet young faces at "circle time" in the classroom where you teach. Maybe it's a huddle of those sweaty kids you coach, a boardroom or breakroom table where you work. Or maybe it's your kitchen table. The Lord will use you in these circles for His glory. Today, may your path cross with someone who needs the love of Christ evidenced in your life and the encouragement and strength He can infuse through you.

The Sifting of a Saint

Praise the Lord, O my soul, and forget not all his benefits – who forgives all your sins, and heals all your diseases, who redeems your life from the pit and crowns you with love and compassion. Psalm 103:2-5 NIV

We can best see the lavish love of Christ from the depths of our shame and destruction. Romans 5:8 tell us that while we were still sinning, Christ shed His blood for us in death. As surely as His lifeblood was necessary for any of us, it was for Peter. His life serves as a testimony of hope. In Luke 22:31-34, we see a discourse between Peter and Jesus when Peter is told that Satan has asked to sift him as wheat. Sifting wheat divides the good and bad, so only the useful grain remains. Why do you think Satan had asked to sift Peter? The sifting would be severe enough to affect his soul, mind, and body, shaking him to the core. The most encouraging news to Peter (if he recognized good news at all) is that Christ had prayed for him (Luke 22:32). In that same scripture, Christ makes sure to mention that Peter will return for a purpose only He can ordain.

We often miss encouragement when it is encased in words that leave us questioning, hurt, or confused. Putting myself in Peter's place, I'd wonder about the sifting. *How is it going to come? Will it be hard on me?* "But I have prayed for you," Jesus said. He also foretold Peter's return, clearly communicating how his life would be used. Whether that rested assuredly on Peter's ears or not, it was fact.

Has Satan ever sifted you as wheat? Do you know why? I've been sifted for my own good. Christ had purpose in my sifting, and I am humbled that He is mindful of me. I recently purchased a book titled *When Godly People Do Ungodly Things* by Beth Moore. At first, it seemed the book would serve no meaning for my life. I did not see how it could apply to me because I was closer to the Lord than I'd ever been before. I didn't escape the bookstore before the Lord seized my attitude. He revealed a self-righteous spirit and imperfect heart. I surrendered guilty as charged and walked out, book in hand.

The timing of a God, who orders the universe, makes the heart beat in perfect rhythm. He causes creation to march to His cadence. He plans opportunities in the lives of His children to make us walk to His step. I learned from and was warned by the stories and scripture references detailed in the pages of a book I had no idea I needed. Peter never imagined that *he* would deny the Lord. He thought the dreaded denial would come from another less committed disciple, but not him. Has the Lord ever rebuked you about an attitude in your heart that was not right before Him?

At this point in the story, Peter didn't know how the sifting would take place. But let's look at Christ's prediction of the denial and the inevitable course of events.

A Deplorable Prediction

Jesus said, "Watch and pray so that you will not fall into temptation. The spirit is willing, but the body is weak." Matthew 26:41 NIV

To the disciples, it was a deplorable prediction to utter that Judas would betray, and Peter would deny. Imagine what they thought. Peter seemed more committed than at least some of the other disciples. He was a zealous leader. He was always the first to speak, but not to think. Let's trace this young leader's footsteps for a few moments and study a second prediction of the denial from Matthew 26:31-35. When a warning comes twice, it can make us fearful. Warnings are to keep us out of harm's way, but so often they don't.

Jesus told Peter and the other disciples they would deny Him, though none of them could fathom it. How many times have we had the opportunity to stand up for Christ, but instead we cower down? Peter appeared strong in his commitment and bold in his love. Perhaps the disciples had a blind love for their Friend, or they did not fully understand their relationship with Christ. They may have envisioned a valiant love, but soon their weaknesses would be glaring before them. Matthew 26:41 gives us hope. The spirit may be willing, but the body is weak. Isn't that what gets us in trouble every time? When our weaknesses are not thrown at the feet of Jesus, we face them continuously with no escape. Jesus used prophecy that confirmed Peter would deny. He quoted from the words of God in Zechariah 13:7, "I will strike the shepherd, and the sheep of the flock will be scattered." Later, the disciples were scattered to serve the gospel to more people groups. This time, the scattering referred to the falling away of the disciples during Jesus' most crucial life struggle. We hear Peter first, "Lord, not me! All the rest might, but I'll never leave you (my paraphrase)!" Oh, the words we wish had never left our lips! The Lord left no room for error. Without the facts, Peter could have easily (yet wrongfully) justified the denial. He made sure Peter would know he had denied his Lord.

    In Matthew 26:31-35 two details describe when the denial would take place. The other disciples said it would never happen, yet they fell away. Peter's heart deceived him. How quickly we are led astray.

    Looking ahead (Matthew 26:36-45), we see Jesus allowed Peter to be closer than most in the garden. Christ never forsakes those He knows will forsake Him. We may reason that Peter's denial was more deplorable than any other. What about us? Christ has never forsaken you and me though we have forsaken Him innumerable times and ways. What love and mercy!

Now, let's peer intently into the deep pit of Peter's denial. What takes place is a perfect parallel to the prophecy from a pure, spotless Lamb.

Warmed by Glowing Embers

Do not put out the Spirit's fire; do not treat prophecies with contempt. Test everything. Hold on to the good. Avoid every kind of evil.
I Thess. 5:19-22 NIV

The temperature rises in Peter's predicament (Luke's 22:54-63). Even though Peter followed at a distance, he *was* following. Comfortable but costly, following at a distance can make us distant followers. I'm convinced it is the last thing Peter wanted to do, become distant and detached.

As soon as they seized Jesus, we see Peter, but where have the others gone? If you had been one of the disciples, would you have been more likely to deny or hide? We have no idea how we might respond in this life-threatening predicament. Many Christians live in eminent danger, though most have no idea what it would be like. Deny or hide. Neither choice is good. Perhaps following at a distance was the only thing Peter knew to do. Not wanting Christ's words to be true, he still feared for his life. To his credit, he went further than the rest as he stepped into the courtyard of the high priest's house. In Luke 22:55 we see what Peter did next. We might have done the same thing, just slip into the crowd hovering close to be "in the know". Then, the moment of recognition comes. As Peter warms by the fire, its glowing embers reveal his identity to those around him.

Verse 56 states that the servant girl looked closely at him. We'd be good Christians if people weren't looking so closely. Figuratively, Peter was standing too close to the fire. Who is looking closely at your life? As they look at your life, they see either the glow from Christ or from the world's fire as you stand close enough to blend in and stay warm. Just as Peter was speaking, the rooster crowed. And Jesus, standing close by, turned and looked straight at Peter. As sharply as the Word made flesh slices, we want the word of the Lord to judge us rather than others (Hebrews 4:12-13). It's exploratory surgery of the best kind. A pure sword can cut into a heart and make it clean. Luke 22:62 tells the end of the denial. Peter wept bitterly.

Though bitter to us, these tears are sweet to the Lord when they are repentant (Psalm 51:7). The Lord requires a heart like this before He can turn a child of God back to Himself. Perhaps Peter wept bitterly because that thing he said would never happen did. In Christ, embers of the Spirit's fire burn, but we must keep vigil that the smoldering ashes of our sinful nature are not easily fanned to flames again. Take a look back at Thessalonians 5:19-22 noted earlier as encouragement to keep the Spirit's embers burning in your life.

2
The Reality of the Present

Reality has a way of settling in on a soul. You've felt it on the last day of a great vacation, or during a two a.m. feeding of a newborn baby you so desperately want to sleep through the night... After moving a house full of furniture (that still must be unpacked)... When you lose someone you dearly love... When rock bottom feels like it, and hope is a distant, forgotten fragment... Jesus had been crucified. Sadly, for the disciples, the present had an absence – the flesh and blood of Jesus Christ. Reality for these men was the loss of a mentor, teacher, brother, and close friend. The very person of Jesus surely was a compelling presence, so much so that the disciples immediately followed Him. But now, He was no longer standing in front of them. Absence leaves a vacancy, a separation we all dread. They could no longer touch the One who had touched them.

Reality is the real stuff of life, where our weaknesses roll out of bed every time we do and our strengths aren't nearly as solid as we thought. The disciples are forced to face reality after Jesus is crucified. John 21 will be our scene's text with Peter and Jesus as main characters. We'll gain a unique perspective with a dash of wonders, still never knowing all the miracles Christ performed. He performs wonders that cannot be fathomed, and miracles that cannot be counted (Job 5:9).

A Morning with the Master

Jesus said to them, "Come and have breakfast." None of the disciples dared ask him, "Who are you?" They knew it was the Lord. John 21:12 NIV

We begin our journey to grasp the primary purpose of Jesus' encounter with Peter and some of the other disciples. The first half of John 21 is our text. Though we're tempted to see the miraculous catch of fish as the only act, instead we'll look with telescopic vision at other equally amazing wonders performed by the Lord. We can often be blind to the truth of Scripture when it's the last thing we want to see. Recently, I heard an old hymn arranged in a new way. Having spent practically every Sunday on a church pew, the words of old hymns often ring in my memory. Let the words of an old hymn by Fanny Crosby become the prayer of your heart.

Savior, Savior, hear my humble cry,
While on others thou art calling, do not pass me by.[1]

We continue with a look at the exchange of brothers in Christ revealed in John 21. Just as the Lord is calling the disciples, He's calling you and me. Just like them, He wants us to come closer and see what we've never seen before. Peter's call takes place in John 21. While on others you are calling, Lord, do not pass us by. Help us hear when you call. I wonder, have you ever heard the Lord calling you in some inaudible, but very clear way?

In John 21:1-14, Jesus appeared again to the disciples. Always appearing again, the Lord provides many opportunities for fellowship. He desires our fellowship as much as we need His. But we must be deliberate in spending time with Him. He will never be an unwelcome guest.

In John 21:3, Peter tells the others he is going out to fish, and they follow. What would you do? Though they had placed their faith in the person of Christ, it seemed now they must go on without Him. We've also been disheartened after great loss. Perhaps death steals a loved one, a beloved pastor resigns, a great boss or friend moves away, or a spouse walks out the door. The past fades fast, the present sadly finds a new normal, and the future is full of uncertainty. In the midst of it all, the disciples who stepped out to follow Christ mustered the motivation to get on with life. Going back to their former trade seemed reasonable. How do you tend to respond to uncertainty in life?

Peter takes this fitting role of leader again, but he is of no effect without Christ at the helm. Haven't we been there? The disciples had seen great miracles, but this night revealed a dark emptiness in their lives, both emotionally and physically. The all-night fishing trip seemed to be of no value, eternal or otherwise.

Early in the morning, Jesus comes on the scene. He shows up right on time, though probably not in their eyes. He appeared when the disciples were tired and hungry, despairing and drained. In the same way, He reveals Himself to us when we are desperate for help. Our nets are empty. Our stomachs are starving. Our bodies are weary. Often the lure to forsake the promises of Christ becomes more inviting at times like these. Why do you think Jesus waited? Has He ever waited until it's almost too late before He acts on your behalf?

Though the disciples did not know it was Jesus, He called out to them. "Friends, haven't you any fish?" Friend. It's our key word for this book. Jesus esteemed them as friends. The words of this praise song relate the unimaginable relationship Christ pursues with us:

> *Your love is extravagant.*
> *Your friendship, intimate.*
> *I find I'm moving to the rhythms of your grace*
> *Your fragrance is intoxicating in our secret place*
> *Your love is extravagant*
> *Spread wide in the arms of Christ*
> *Is the love that covers sin*

*No greater love have I ever known
You'd consider me a 'friend'
capture my heart again²*

At what time in your life have you realized that the Lord is your intimate Friend? Christ called to His friends with a question about fish. But when He asks, these purposeful questions both provoke and deserve honest answers. We can answer however we choose, though He always knows the truth. The relationship He seeks merits the truth, even if it's not too spiritual. May we never leave unanswered a question from the Lord.

An Abundant Catch

*He said, "Throw your net on the right side of the boat
and you will find some."
John 21:6 NIV*

When Jesus makes a command, it's far more than a suggestion. The disciples soon discover this first hand. After a long night of unsuccessful fishing, the disciples caught a glimpse of an unidentified man standing at the water's edge when dawn broke. From a distance, he commanded them to cast their nets on the right side of the ship. After catching a multitude of fish, Peter and the others realized that this man must be their Lord.

Immediate obedience is a key element. Be inclined to err on the side of faith when you believe Christ has given you a direct command. It's always a better choice than disobedience. Ask yourself, 'Does this command agree with scripture?' This is the most important acid test. Reason it any other way and you will figure a reason not to obey. If what has been whispered in your spirit lines up with scripture, then why not line up and obey? When we begin to obey immediately and consistently, our nets will soon be full, and we'll lose count of the miracles God is working in and through us.

How often have you heard a voice speaking to your heart, but you did not realize it was Jesus? Listen for Him to speak. If you wait expectantly, you will be more likely to realize that it is your Master speaking.

Peter's passion is worth noting in John 21:7-8. As soon as John told Peter who it was, he plunged into the water. His limbs moved swiftly in life-saving valiance, but this time He was swimming toward the One who had saved him. It was John who discerned the Savior, but Peter who leapt with the passion to respond. We need to pray for both discernment and desire. Without discernment, we will not know the voice of the Lord. Without desire, we will not have the fervency to promptly obey. Scripture tells us the other disciples followed. Are you a leader or a follower? Why do you think it would be important to share with others, as John did, what you believe the Lord has spoken to you?

Both leaders and followers are needed in the body of Christ. Whatever Christ calls you to, be faithful. He will be clear when He speaks. If it's not clear, then wait and pray. Many have asked the Lord to confirm what He has spoken. For one example, see Judges 6:17-39. You may also choose to speak with another discerning Christian about what has been impressed on you. He or she may encourage you, point you to scripture, or warn you. With whom are you able to openly share about what God is doing in your life?

In John 21:9-10, we see that the disciples pulled the boat onto land and they saw a fire of burning coals on the shore. Jesus was there, ready and waiting with fish, bread, and burning coals, He set the table for them just as He does for you and me. Though He provides everything we need at the table of fellowship, Christ still invites us to bring something to serve. He wants our offering, our gift. He gives us every opportunity. He has gifted us with everything we bring to Him yet we often hold our catch of fish captive in our nets. You possess your gift, and only you can offer it. What gift do you hold in your hands?

In comparing John 21:11 to verse 6, Jesus said they'd find "some" (verse 6). Why was it so important to John to record in verse 11 that there were 153 large fish? Was it to support the accuracy and credibility of the story? Record the Lord's work in your life as accurately as John recorded this miracle. As others read it, perhaps they'll learn from it as we are learning from John's account. What work has the Lord done in your life that is large and exact?

Neat Netting

> ...but even with so many (fish) the net was not torn.
> John 21:11b NIV

We continue in John 21 as we see that when the Lord performs a miracle, He manages to work out the details too. It's hard to imagine how He'll take care of the intricacies that often overwhelm us. First, in John 21:6, they were unable to haul (or lift) the net because of the abundance of fish. But the net was not torn.

The work the Lord entrusts to us can seem like a staggering responsibility, but your net will not be torn. Great is your reward. When service becomes an obligation, we have lost sight of the One we serve. If we volunteer to do many things, we might miss the one thing we were set apart to do for His glory. After hard lessons, the Spirit now checks my motive before I take on any act of service. Service can be the enemy of true servanthood. We have been raised in a self-centered society. Do we desire more to meet our needs or help meet the needs of others? In what way are you currently serving that seems burdensome (inside or outside the church)?

Every year, the managing director of the YMCA Blue Ridge Assembly at Black Mountain, NC speaks to many groups about serving. As he welcomes our particular group on opening night, he tells that the staff's mission to serve is an act of dignity. Whether they are cleaning a guest room, washing dishes or babysitting, it's still dignified. I once saw a babysitter with a child who had become ill. This teenage girl faced the unpleasant experience of a child vomiting all over her as she waited for the child's mother to return. Though she may not have felt dignified at the time, what the director said is right. Doing is dignified. Serving others is serving God. Your net will not be torn. We want to move away from considering where we are of use and toward becoming a servant who can be used. In Luke 22:27 *NIV*, Christ tells us at least one motivation to serve. *For who is greater, the one who is at the table or the one who serves? Is it not the one who is at the table? But I am among you as one who serves (NIV).* If Christ's primary role was to serve, ours is as well – in whatever way we are gifted to do so.

As is His way, Jesus said, "Come and have breakfast" (John 21:12). How many friends would join you for breakfast? Barely awake and without a few cups of coffee, some of us aren't morning people. Look back at John 21:4. It was early when He called them. He invites us to be with Him early. You won't search scripture long to find Christ rising early to spend time with God the Father in prayer. Even on resurrection day, His glorified body was raised up early! What is early for you? He speaks in the morning hours, before we get too busy to listen. He wants to commune with us before we have an opportunity to get frustrated at a single soul. When my three children were young, it *had* to be early. Sleepy eyes, bed head hair, and stumbling staggers are priceless to me, but I had to rise early to let the Lord speak to me before I spoke to them. I'll never forget the times my children have caught me on my knees. Like little warriors, they would get right down beside me and bow their heads. I pray the Father will catch them doing the same thing. Consider when you spend time with the Lord. What is your routine, just the two of you? What, if anything, would you like to do differently regarding your time with Him?

If you have not committed to a consistent quiet time, why not begin today? Ask the Lord to help you carve out the best time. He'll bless your diligence and discipline no matter what time fits your routine. It's a sacrificial act of submission to the Lord.

Glorious Appearances

Now this was the third time Jesus appeared to his disciples after he was raised from the dead. John 21:14 NIV

Let's share some more time in the richness and texture of John 21, and look at some glorious appearances and revelations. It's rewarding to unravel the mysteries in scripture. As we weave the related subjects and passages together, we'll learn from Jesus by the Spirit revealing truth to us. At this point, Christ had appeared to the disciples three times since the resurrection. How did the first two appearances compare to the third? When you read John 20, you'll take in the entire account of Christ's first two appearances.

Again, we see John and Peter in a competitive spirit (John 20:4-9). They both ran, but one had enough fortitude to race right into the tomb. That would be our friend, Peter. The scene reveals personality traits about these disciples that make them more like us. We tend to rank them a cut above the other disciples (see John 20:8b). However, the only difference between us and any of them is we are blessed even more because we have not seen, but still believe (John 20:29).

We walk by faith. We struggle to understand the simplicity of the gospel, much less the complexity. The blood has become precious. The resurrection has become hope. They saw and believed. Our spiritual eyes can see *and* believe, as it is revealed to us. Praise the Lord! In John 20:19-20, Christ first appears to the disciples. The disciples were behind locked doors fearing for their lives. He knew this and entered to relate to their great need for peace, at the very least.

Speaking emphatically to their need, He did not come in and stand among them saying, "You are in fear, and I am patience," or "You are in fear, so I am kindness." He came to them as Peace. Patience is good. Kindness is nice. But when I am afraid, it is peace that stills my fear. Peace in this passage is *eirene* in Greek. The word is probably from a primary verb eiro (to join); peace (literally or figuratively); by implication prosperity; - one, peace, quietness, rest, + set at one again.[3] When Christ gives peace, I can rest. The following scriptures concerning peace will be helpful to you if you'll make time to let the Lord speak to you through His Word: Isaiah 9:6-7; Ephesians 2:14; and Colossians 3:15.

From behind locked doors, Christ penetrated through to take captive their fears. He made entrance not to bring peace, but to *be* their Peace. As this Prince is our Peace, He also has rule in our hearts. When we allow the ruling authority of Christ to enter our fearful situations, we can know peace and be at rest. Glorious about this appearing is when the Lord came as Peace, the disciples found joy as an added wonder. John tells us in verse 20 that "the disciples were overjoyed when they saw the Lord." True peace brings great joy. At times, we struggle to find peace. We'd be satisfied with just enough to get us through a sleepless night or a fearful situation. Later, when we realize the Prince of Peace entered our hearts, joy is a natural response. Next, we'll look at one more friend in scripture who, no doubt, saw the Lord.

Unless I See Him

Then he said to Thomas, "Put your finger here; see my hands. Reach out your hand and put it into my side. Stop doubting and believe!" John 20:27 NIV

Thomas made a statement to the disciples when they told him about seeing the resurrected Savior. "Unless I see the nail marks in his hands and put my finger where the nails were, and put my hand into his side, I will not believe it." (John 20:25 NIV)

Doubting Thomas is not the best nickname when you consider the end of the story. Again, one disciple is an example for the rest of us. The Lord will grant even our unspoken requests. When our spoken and unspoken requests match His desires, He'll grant them in due time. What has the Lord accomplished in your life in "the wait" for your need to be answered?

When the Lord entered again to the locked room, He did not say to Thomas, "Take a look - it's me." Instead, Jesus told him to do exactly what Thomas had earlier said would transform his unbelieving heart (John 20:25). He used Thomas' own request to change him. Christ spoke his language. He offered his side and his hands.

Christ removed the doubt from the doubter. As belief filled his heart, his mouth exclaimed, "My Lord and my God!" The issue was settled. Having felt the scars with his hands and seen them with his eyes, Thomas had his previous request granted – a request that would help him believe in a Savior who wasn't present in the flesh to even hear it.

Even those who saw Christ face to face had trouble believing, just like we do. Even those who knew the scripture and were looking for the Messiah didn't realize He was right before their eyes. Stop doubting and believe, for one day we shall see Him. No appearance we have studied will be as awesome as the one yet to come. We will be changed, in the twinkling of an eye (I Cor. 13:12). As we close this chapter, remember:

- Jesus often comes on the scene when our backs are against the wall. His specialty is working in our lives when nothing else will. Consider what or who you can give to Him that you've practically given up on as of late.
- When we give Jesus what we hold in our hands, He will work miracles that are large and exact. Record those miracles in a personal journal. Give God the glory.
- When serving the Lord becomes an obligation, we have lost sight of the One we serve. We are to return to the One we serve daily to be refreshed, recharged, and refocused.
- When Christ appears to us, He meets us at our need. For the disciples, fear subsided when Peace came in through locked doors. Consider what doors you have locked in your life. Christ will penetrate them to release you from captivity.
- Stop doubting and believe. Believe Jesus is able to save you. Believe He is able to satisfy your requests to see Him face to face.

Jesus appeared to His friends, not only during His years of ministry but also in His glorified body. He made sure those most needing to see Him did. Friendship with Jesus requires faith. Doubt loomed in their eyes. Jesus filled their empty nets. This Prince of Peace calmed their fears. He answered their requests. He is all we need. No other friend compares. No other relationship matches this one.

3
The Purpose of the Future

Have you ever known someone who always had a plan? Meet me. I would schedule the spontaneity out of life if my husband would let me! I pray Proverbs 19:21 regularly, "Lord, many are the plans of my heart, but let it be so that only your purpose prevails." Jeremiah pronounced the word of the Lord to the Israelites when he said, "For I know the plans I have for you," declares the Lord, "plans to prosper you and not to harm you, plans to give you a hope and a future" (Jeremiah 29:11). The Lord had a purpose for Peter's life, just as He does for you and me.

Let's wade out into the water where the boat and the net full of fish were both dragged ashore in John 21. It's the same water that rushed onto the shore where Jesus stood calling out to His friends. Let's stand in it ankle deep for a while and cool our feet. As we listen to the soft roar of the waves rolling in, we'll be calm knowing that the Prince of Peace is with us, teaching us with His words, the catch and a hot breakfast. From this view, just at the water's edge, we'll be able to hear the exchange between Christ and the one disciple He connected with to teach and draw to Himself. Perhaps the Lord will use this passage to draw us in the same way.

An Unfinished Breakfast

"Lord, you know all things; you know that I love you."
John 21:17b NIV

A meal with friends is just beginning when the plates are empty. The best part is always the visit. We find the disciples having breakfast with the Master. We join them on the seashore in John 21:15, where they had taken their last bites.

Christ will always feed us if we are willing to give Him the time to serve us. How often do we urge our children or grandchildren to eat when they are hard at play? At times, they certainly don't want to be spoon-fed, much less take time to feed themselves. We are the same way - so busy. Children are often on a short fuse when they haven't eaten, but we know they must. If we can't stop to let the Master serve us a regular diet of spiritual food, we are too busy. If we have not cared enough to feed ourselves, then we are too carefree.

It takes time to sit and be nourished instead of waiting until struggles come your way to allow the Master to feed you. Do this in the quietness of life, in the "daily-ness" of life. When the struggles come, it's unfortunate but true - you will only be strengthened emotionally to the extent you have sustained yourself spiritually. Perhaps you have faced a hard time, physically or mentally. The mind and body are too faint to sit at the feet of Jesus and learn of Him. The distractions are overwhelming. During these times, it's the hardship itself that is served up to teach. It's difficult to walk by faith and even more difficult to be a testimony to others.

This passage is a "show and tell" for at least one disciple. Jesus has a word with Peter over a good hot breakfast about feeding others. It's as if the others bury themselves in the sand while Peter comes to the forefront. When Jesus picks you or me out from the crowd, He has something of great value to teach us. Can you think of a time or circumstance where you felt the Lord picking you out from others?

In John 21, Christ asks Peter something very specific in this passage. In the Greek, there are several different words for our word 'love'. We will deal with two of them: *agape*, which is a volitional, self-sacrificial love and *phileo* signifying affection, affinity, or brotherly love.[4] Think of it this way. Agape love is in the best interest of another, where *phileo* love is in common interest with another.

First, Christ asks Peter, "Do you truly *agape* love me more than these?" This is self-sacrificial love, but Peter responds, "Yes, you know that I *phileo* love you." His answer affirms friendship love. I've placed the kind of love in italics with each reference to help us see the point more clearly.

This dialogue reminds me of my kids! I ask a simple question, but get an unexpected, unclear answer. Surely, my child understands the question. Getting the truth is not always easy. Christ intends to finally receive the truth from Peter's heart.

Once again, we find Christ full of purposeful questions. He will continue asking us the same questions until honesty surfaces. He already knows the truth, all the while it is the Lord's intention to reveal the truth *He* knows to us. If you are like me (and Peter), you have discovered that Christ has a way of revealing something to you about yourself which you did not realize. In the passage, Jesus replies to Peter's answer with a command, "Then feed my lambs."

Again in John 21:16, Jesus asked, "Simon, son of John, do you *agape* love me?" Peter answered, "Yes, Lord, you know that I *phileo* love you." A similar reply came from Jesus: "Then take care of my sheep." Christ makes simple commands, but He'll make them repeatedly until we are ready to obey. Prepare your heart for immediate obedience.

Questions with a Cause

Peter was hurt because Jesus asked him the third time, "Do you love me?" John 21:17b

When the same question is asked of you time and again, it can be quite frustrating. In reviewing John 21:15-19, it would seem the same line of questioning would be getting old to Peter. And it was. But he was as slow to understand as we sometimes are. The third time, the same question was asked, but it was repeated in a slightly different way.

Agape love was replaced with *phileo* love in the question Jesus asked Peter: "Simon, son of John, do you *phileo* love me?" Until this time, Jesus asked whether Peter loved Him in a sacrificial way while Peter kept confirming his friendship love for the Lord. But this time, Jesus asked him in the way Peter had been answering all along, as if to say, "Peter, you've been saying you friendship love me. Do you *really* friendship love me?" or "Are you *even* my friend?" It's a good thing the writer (John) was discerning the non-verbal exchange, or we'd have missed much of the context of this dialogue. Peter seemed to be insulted that Christ kept asking him the same question. He did not realize Christ's intentionality of love in the repetitiveness. Surely, it's no accident that Christ allowed Peter to vow his love for the Lord the same number of times Peter had previously denied Him...three.

A clear act of forgiveness and reconciliation, Jesus invited Peter to proclaim his love three times. A deliberate denial hardly deserves a merciful makeup. But it's the exchange we would each long for from the Son of God. Peter was hurt, John writes, because Jesus asked him the third time. Peter's response, "Lord, you know all things; you know that I love you." So true, the Lord does know all things. He knows more about our lives than we know ourselves (see Ps. 33:13-15; 56:8; and 121).

Ah, Peter answered correctly. The Lord does know all things, and He loves us anyway. He allowed Peter the privilege of proclaiming his love thrice. That's about as deliberate as I can fathom. If any of the disciples needed this ministry of love, mercy and grace, it was Peter. The water we're wading in right now at the edge of that seashore might be cool, but my heart is warm. A fresh wave rolls in over my feet as I sit at His. What a lavish love He offers!

Lastly, Jesus gave the same command as a third and final response, "Feed my sheep." How can we apply this to our own lives if we don't understand it? Is it practical? Is it applicable? A sheep myself, I also need feeding, but Christ calls us to feed *His* sheep. We are disciples called to make disciples, but how do we apply this command today in our busy lives?

Christ was nourishing the disciples with the fish He had provided and prepared. Jesus offers a timely illustration to these men. The Good Shepherd is literally feeding the disciples, yet encouraging them to feed others, spiritually, at the very least.

The command Christ gave Peter was quite simple, "Feed my sheep". But He gave the command three times. Why? Surely the Shepherd was making a point with Peter and the others He did not want them to miss. What did He mean, "Feed my sheep"? We'll use scripture to draw some conclusions. Let's take time to graze the pastures of God's Word to learn of Him, to be fed and satisfied. How can this be? You are being fed by God's Word. For that, be thankful.

If I'm not deliberately feeding myself (spiritually or physically), I am cranky, anxious and miserable. I can't think about anything else, except how hungry or empty I am. An empty heart also hungers for something to fill it.

"Blessed are those who hunger and thirst for righteousness, for they will be filled.
Matthew 5:6 NIV

Has your heart ever been hungry? Thirsty? Look with me at some passages which explain why the heart can be hungry, and how the Lord can satisfy that emptiness. I adore the book of Hosea because the Lord proclaims His love in such extravagant, gracious ways through this story. The literary work described the children of Israel, if not so stubborn, as lambs in a meadow (Hosea 4:16). That picturesque scene would hang beautifully above my mantle. So serene and well-tended, I can imagine plump little lambs grazing on lush green hills. The sunset in the background would be spread like a tablecloth across the sky. The Lord makes many promises to the hungry heart, even to the hungry stomach. Some are found in Psalm 17:14b, Isaiah 55:1-2, and Matthew 5:6. Our Shepherd wants us to give Him our hungry hearts. He wants to feed us from His pastures free of charge! The question becomes: Are we willing to be fed? Or will we be like some of our children? Too busy.

Too many to count are the times we've gathered around on Sunday at my in-laws after morning worship. We've enjoyed some of the best country cookin' you've ever put in your mouth. While we're cleaning up, someone will always say, "This will be my last meal for the day." It never is. We're always hungry again by suppertime!

No doubt, there are many other passages we could study regarding this reality. The Lord has purpose in our dissatisfaction with not only food, but also material goods, power, wealth and other things that are temporary satisfiers. He intends for us to search until we find what truly feeds and fills the hunger in our hearts.

It's increasingly difficult in today's society to be drawn to a place of still and quiet long enough to be fed by the Word of God. We'd rather go to worship and be fed, or get the essentials in Sunday school, and these ways are good. From the aspect of physical hunger, we don't want to invest much time and energy in either. The fast food, instant, microwaveable stuff is just fine with most of us. But eating really nutritious food (spiritually or physically) takes more time, more stillness, and more preparation.

My mother loved studying Scripture, and that planted a seed in me. She would sit for hours, read her Bible, pray, or even listen to preaching on cassette tape. She passed away when I was 18, but many seeds had been planted in my life by that time. Even so, I did not complete my first Bible study until I was 25 and married. Then, it was years before I picked up another one. Life got busier. Oh, the people who long for one or two pages of God's Word, yet the dust settles on five or more Bibles of our own for all sorts of reasons.

During the early years of marriage, Gary and I had started our careers and were working, raising a family, building a home, and attending church. We were faithful to do all of that. Wasn't it enough? One day, a long-distance friend planted one more seed. She asked me to do a Bible study on the Internet with her.

It was a 10-week Bible study that took this working mother of three young children twice that long to complete. The Lord promises that His Word will not return void, and will accomplish what it is sent forth to do. I remember the appropriate subtitle of the study: *An Explosion of Faith*. I'm still exploding. It took a lot of sowing by others and a commitment of time before I began to love God's Word. Early on, I realized what I was missing. Being fed has advantages and blessings that we cannot fathom until we take time to allow the Lord to spread the tablecloth, bring out the fine china and crystal, and prepare a feast for just one. He can do that, you know? I pray you will ask the Good Shepherd now to make your heart the sweet dwelling place for His Word in a way that would transform your life into His likeness more every day. Next, we'll take a look at how good ole' soul food can really make the difference in the life of any Christian. The revelation of the good news of the gospel can make a life-saving difference. If you aren't sure of your salvation, pray. Take time to talk with someone you know can help you understand what it means to be saved. This is the most important decision you will ever face in life, bar none.

Soul Food

"I have heard the grumbling of the Israelites. Tell them, 'At twilight you will eat meat and in the morning you will be filled with bread. Then you will know that I am the Lord your God.' Exodus 16:12 NIV

My own explosion of faith, I confess, was not one massive event. But I do vividly remember the moment I realized, "This is what I've been missing!" I knew I had finally found it - the transforming Word of God. For years, I thought it was a more liberating praise and worship service that I needed. I'm an expressive person. I may be able to hide a particular emotion from the outside world, but those who know me well can tell when something is wrong, or even when something is right! If I have to, I'll lift my hands to praise in my car. I love to worship when and where I feel liberty. But that wasn't it. I thought the missing link was prayer for a time in my life, but I discovered that was not all that was missing.

Through my spiritual journey, I'd been missing a good many things. In fact, I was going through the motions as I attended church, but I seldom prayed on my own in the privacy of a quiet time with the Lord. I had no idea what true worship was. I thought it had something to do with the music and the expression of praise outwardly and corporately. Now, I know that worship is more an attitude of the heart. Not only is worship a corporate experience of singing praises, it's also what we do every time we sincerely study the Word, pray, talk with someone about the Lord, and as we simply meditate on the good things of the Lord in the quiet places of our hearts. Worship is more than a structured program in a corporate setting.

During these times of searching, wonderful things have happened. I have learned to worship in the attitude of my heart. I've come to understand the power of an effective prayer life. The Lord has instilled a passionate love for His Word in me.

This poem is my testimony of how the Lord has shown me one more missing link in my walk with Him. Perhaps you have found it too! The Word – it's quick, and powerful, and sharper than any two-edged sword, piercing even to dividing soul and spirit, joints and marrow, and is a discerner of the thoughts and intents of the heart (Heb. 4:12 NIV).

Dwelling Place

I can't remember what day it was
when I opened up His Word,
And realized there was so much more
than what I'd ever heard.
A Christian from my childhood, now a mother too,
God had been faithful, still I didn't have a clue.

The first Bible, my parents placed it in my hand,
Two more I'd bought with hopes to better understand.
One was for the car, one was for the church bench,
The firist? Just in case I needed to use it in a pinch.
I never understood why Mom loved to read His Word.
I'd see her every morning and think,
"She must be really bored."

Now, things are different, but His Word hasn't changed.
Somewhere along the way, my thoughts were rearranged.
See I've become an addict, I'm ready to admit.
In this path called life, His Word – it is my fix.

Sometimes I let things go I think need my attention,
Because I get so engrossed in His God-sized intentions.
Then I stop and thank this great big God of mine,
"Surely Lord, again today, please redeem the time!"

You see, He's given me a hunger and nothing else will do.
His Word is breath to me, it's life, it's power too.
It's richer fare than you've ever had before
And will leave you, after tasting, only wanting more.

It's changed the way I see myself, the way I look at life.
He's changing the way I am, the friend, mother, wife.
It's changed the way I choose to live,
He's changing my life.

I wonder if I'll have the time before He calls me to depart,
To tell everyone one I can
just what His words mean to my heart.

Here's a great offer, a lifetime guarantee –
Read His Word, ask Him to show you all there is to see.
His Spirit dwelling within you will shine a searching light
Revealing mysteries and wonders,
bringing bright light to the darkness of night.

The Word become flesh and dwelt among us –
the strangest thing to see.
And so amazing still –
His Word now is dwelling deep inside of me!
Mel Ann Sullivan 2004

What kinds of foods do you like? I love the local Mexican Restaurant. I also enjoy the Peking Buffet. But I crave soul food from Scripture. I know if I've missed my daily intake. There are healthy benefits to a regular diet of soul food. We'll look at a few of them. One of the things I love about this spiritual food is the variety. Leftovers don't spoil. It's kind of like potato salad or turnips, better on the second day! The table is never bare, and you can always go back for another helping. I push back from His banqueting table after feasting, and I know I'll be back for more, just never quickly enough. When is the last time you had a good filling? Don't wait too long.

Bountiful Benefits

Take a look at what the Scriptures say about the benefits of taking in a regular diet of soul food:
#1 - You will know that the Lord is God (Ex. 16:12).

#2 – You will find favor and understanding from God and man (Proverbs 3:1-5).

#3 – God's Word will be sweet to your soul, and you will be able to speak truth to others (Ezekiel 3:3-4).

#4 – You will be satisfied at God's hand (Matthew 6:26).

#5 – The bread of life will both satisfy your hunger and quench your thirst (John 6:35).

If you haven't experienced each of these benefits, ask the Lord to make them real for you. He is faithful, and He will do it.

Being well-fed is a wonderful thing. We must always submit to the deliberate act of feeding ourselves, even as we grow strong in faith. Maturity in Christ is marked by the humble act of daily obedience in being fed, regardless of age or years of commitment to the Lord. So, pull up to the table for a helping of soul food that you will not feel guilty about later! And if you don't like spiders, brace yourself to learn from one little spider that knows how to feed itself.

A Spider Story

Think about feeding yourself like the spider does. Gary and I have watched a spider spin her web. First, she made several heavy duty lines of support from sturdy objects. Second, she began to network those lines together to a center point. She took time at the center to make sure the knitting was strongly reinforced. Then, she wove her first outside circle, after which she attached lines in equal places back to the center. She began to make inner circles spaced apart a wider distance. She then began to fill in with smaller lines in between, only after the pattern had been established. Do not be deceived. A spider does not "sit a spell" to spin. I watched as she used one leg to reach and measure how much line she would need to connect. She scurried to measure every time. The closer she got to the center of the web where she had reinforced it all, the more intricate the lines. In fact, it took the little spider longer to weave the smaller area close to the center than it did to weave the first and larger perimeter of the web.

We didn't think she was done. We could have shown her some places that we thought she may have missed. But she laid herself on the center of that web, waited for her nightly feeding, and rested. She had toiled a good 30 minutes at a very speedy pace to do her spinning. It was tight. It was with such precision, and each step was purposeful. How does she know, we wondered? Is it instinct or intellect that she knows exactly how to feed herself?

I learned as I sat a spell and watched that spider spin. The Lord is good to teach us in ways we'd never imagine. We too weave a web in life. I woke up the next morning with these thoughts and that spider's web still on my mind. Perhaps the strong support lines in our lives are prayer, worship, fellowship, and service. I thought of the little lines that make the circle as daily Bible study because without the little lines, the spider will not be able to feed herself, nor will we. The closer she got to the center (or the heart), the more important it was to weave tighter lines. As she laid her body on the center, it seemed she was protecting it. She knew if the center broke from a flying insect, the entire web would lose strength and fall apart. Unlike the spider, it's difficult for us to place a guard on our center, the heart. We have been instructed differently. It is the peace of God that will guard our hearts and minds through Christ Jesus (Phil. 4:7).

A big lesson from a little spider: She was deliberate about each step she took. And she'll weave using those same steps every time. It is her way of life. It is the way she feeds herself. It's not some random act when she is starving. She doesn't wait until that moment. Whether it's intellect or instinct, she acts according to it every day. This, my friend, is a savvy spider. She's smart and sensible. Though the spider and any remains of the web she spun were gone the next morning, I have a feeling she was well-fed and had been satisfied.

The Host with the Most

Jesus said, "Take care of my sheep. John 21:16b NIV

I have fond memories of my Mom. She was definitely the "hostess with the mostest". Her degree qualified her to teach home economics, which she did for several years. She loved to entertain, and I don't mean just firing up the grill. Mom knew how to prepare the table and the food for a fine dining experience. Let's look at Christ as the Host with the Most who invites us to not only feed at His table, but also to bring others to the feast.
Christ told Peter, "Feed my lambs…Take care of my sheep." The original Greek meanings will be helpful in understanding what this command means. The word

"feed" in John 21:15 and 17 means to pasture, fodder, graze, keep and feed.[5] The word from which "take care" is derived (tend) in John 21:16 means to tend as a shepherd (or figuratively, as a supervisor), to feed (as in cattle), to rule.[6]

    I don't know about you, but my flesh often wants to sink to the lowest place of responsibility when I read the Word. I will be quick to say, "That doesn't apply to me." In some cases, it's true. But the disciples were commanded to go out and make disciples. You may or may not be a preacher, or even a teacher. But you *are* a disciple if you are a Christian. Discipleship starts at the place of one-on-one, everyday encounters with others. The position of disciple brings with it the responsibility of a disciple to "feed" and "tend". Don't mistake it. Don't let your flesh, Satan, or this world talk you out of it. You are made worthy by the blood of the Lamb to "feed" lambs in the way God has gifted you. You are made competent as a minister of the gospel (II Corinthians 3:5-6). So, let's look at what happens when we begin to serve up the gospel to those around us. There are blessings for those who are served, as well as those who are serving at the table of the gospel. Here are a few bountiful benefits of "feeding and tending":

- Encouragement to others (Prov. 10:21)
- Nourishment and peace (Isaiah 14:30)
- Healing, protection, and restoration (Isaiah 58:6-11)
- Blessings of heaven (Matthew 25:31-40)
- Leading others to salvation (Acts 20:25-27)
- A crown of never-ending glory and honor (I Peter 5:2-4)

    Who is entrusted to you to feed or tend? Pray now and ask the Lord to make you aware of opportunities to serve up the gospel in encouraging, teaching, sharing, giving, loving and caring ways. Let's retrace our steps looking back at Peter's last encounter with the glorified Christ on this earth, what it meant for him, and how it applies to our lives.

Tracing Our Steps

The first and last words to Peter by Christ were, "follow me." (See Mark 1:16-17 and John 21:18-22). However, his central purpose of life was to strengthen others to do the same – follow Christ. Peter never failed to follow, even though he stumbled on the path many times. He was even found following as Christ was being led to His death. He was close enough to Christ that the servant girl identified him as a follower. He did not hide, even though he was picked out as a follower and then denied knowing Him. In summary:

- Jesus asked Peter whether he loved Him three times. He will continue to ask the same questions until we are able to honestly answer them. Consider the questions Jesus has asked you. Pray for His help in giving honest answers.
- Ultimately Jesus inquired about Peter's love for Him as a friend. He allowed this disciple to revoke the earlier denial three times over. Christ forgives over and over. He loves over and over. He knows us inside and out. He loves us still.
- We want to have hungry hearts. We want hearts that hunger and thirst for righteousness, for God promises we will be filled. Ask God to make your heart the sweet dwelling place for His Word.
- There are benefits beyond measure to being fed from the Word. However, dangers are facing us if we ever feel we've had enough. A daily dose of soul food from Scripture is the best source of nutrition for believers.

- Peter was given a command to feed the sheep of Jesus. The command is for us as much as it is to us. We must feed our own hungry hearts with God's Word before we can feed others.

Friendship Footprints

Jesus asked Peter to be His friend. Friendship with Christ, however, requires obedience to follow in His steps, and obey His commands. Jesus had befriended Peter, but now He asked Peter to befriend Him. What would it mean? How could Peter possibly measure up? What an intimate relationship we see developing in Scripture. Becoming Christ's friend is a privilege, an honor. Far more, it's a huge responsibility to walk this closely with Christ. However, a journey with this Friend is the sweetest of all. As you go about your days, think of your relationship with Christ. Let Him ask for your hand of friendship. Next, we'll start on a new path and look at some personal testimonies about Christ's relationship with us as friends.

4
Befriend Who?

Where can I go from your Spirit?
Where can I flee from your presence? Ps. 139:7 NIV

Peter had many encounters with the Lord that would be eternally etched into his memory. Could it be that Christ's connection with him that day on the seashore was the one that forever changed him? Some people call them milestones. Others call them stepping stones or landmarks that change the landscape of a life. In the last three chapters, we've focused on pivotal places in Peter's life. Perhaps we've felt this disciple's discouragement as he fished all night but caught nothing. With our lips almost tasting the salty sea water, we dove in with Peter and swam to the shore. Maybe his passion has rubbed off on us. From a distance, we watched as Christ interacted with those disciples, especially Peter, one last time. With John 21 as the plank, let's plunge into the water once more to apply the Scripture to our lives.

Christ had been crucified. To these disciples, He was gone for all practical purposes. They didn't know if or when they'd see Him again. Those who had followed Him were going too, going on with life as it had been before this Jesus captivated their hearts and souls.

Jesus has captivated my heart too. Having been richly satisfied, I have experienced great contentment from studying the Word. Time alone with the Lord has the power to add a new level of intimacy to anyone's spiritual journey, and awakens a hunger we may not otherwise know existed. Even today, my faith is increasing exponentially. The words of Scripture are often timely for the situations I face in a given day, week, or season of life. Isn't that more than I could expect? An intimate encounter with the living

Christ can captivate us. We are least expecting to sense His presence when, at once, He is there. Like Peter's encounter on the seashore, February 20, 2004 will be eternally etched into my life. Though it took me by surprise, I pray that what the Lord taught me will be a surprising delight to you as well.

February 20, 2004 started like any other day. Gary and my boys were off to school. My youngest, Breanna, was home with me. She was always so sweet to entertain herself while I spent time with the Lord. When we have a "holy hush" moment, we are wise to listen and take in all that occurs during that time. Have you ever noticed the Lord will choose anytime to speak, no matter what you may be doing or where you may be? In Jeremiah 33:3, the Lord tells Jeremiah, "Call to me and I will answer you and tell you great and unsearchable things you do not know." Always in touch with us, the Lord chooses His ways of speaking based on how we will best listen and respond. The Lord will speak to your spirit, whether through His Word, His people, circumstances, or creation. This was a moment in my life that God made sure I would never forget.

Holy Hush Moments

Psalm 19:1-4 tells that creation will declare the glory of the Lord. Take a chance to view some shots of constellations and galaxies taken from the famed Hubble Telescope (www.hubblesite.org). Until recent years, no eye has been able to capture these sites. The glory of the Lord will amaze us every time we take a moment to look.

My husband has been working on a one-man project for quite some time. Well, he's always working on a one-man project! He loves our little slice of wildlife paradise just across the state line in Mississippi. He and his father built a simple camp house on the land several years back, and then he added a room, but he did the job alone one board and nail at a time. As he finished his work one day, he deliberately put away his tools and cleaned up just before sunset so he could take it in. Some sunsets are stolen by the clouds, but he couldn't have picked a better day to catch it. It changed the landscape of the sky every minute or so. The colors were magnificent – powdery pink, orchid purple, and every hue of orange you can imagine. He'd never seen one so beautiful. He sat, admiring his own accomplishments too, since he'd almost completed the project. He was proud of the way it had turned out. The Lord spoke to his spirit in that sunset: *"Don't feel bad for having pride in what you've created. But every time you look at the sunset, remember that your creativity is a drop in the bucket compared to mine."*

    Knowing the Lord had spoken to him, he was awestruck. *"Just look at what I can paint for you."* His heart swelled with joy, and his eyes filled with tears. He was humbled by God's voice. Sadly, I missed the scene that day. I asked the Lord the next morning to speak to him in every sunset! Even creation will declare the glory of the Lord. When has the Lord last spoken something to your heart through creation?

    The Lord has spoken to me through His creation, and through other means. But let me get back to the story I promised to share. February 20, 2004 was a mild winter day. I had been studying *On Mission with God* by Henry Blackaby which takes students through the lives of "Mentors for the Journey". Peter was my mentor for the week…over-zealous Peter… foot-in-mouth Peter…yes, also *upon this rock* Peter.

    The scripture reading for the day was John 21, our journey in this book up to now. I knew the routine. A series of questions prompts students to dig deeper after reading Scripture. All was going as planned.

As I read, the Lord began to reveal some truths to me. I've shared some of what was illuminated anew that day. Immediately, I was aware that a strong sense of His presence was presiding over me, from the top of my head to the inmost places of my heart. I was compelled to worship. I was in good company along with David and others who have sensed the same presence, "Where can I go from your Spirit? Where can I flee from your presence? If I go up to the heavens, you are there; if I make my bed in the depths, you are there. If I rise on the wings of the dawn, if I settle on the far side of the sea, even there your hand will guide me, your right hand will hold me fast (Psalm 139:7-10 NIV)."

We may not always be able to sense Him, though we can know that the Lord is always with us. His favor will rest on you and me every time we bow in prayer, take time in the Word, worship, serve, or simply relax in believing He is who He says He is. Honestly, I'm not sure our hearts could stand such a marvelous and more obvious presence very often. However, when we strongly sense He is with us, it is important to be reverent and listen for the reason. Would you take time now to read all of Psalm 139, and be blessed?

He Makes the Call

I keep asking that the God of our Lord Jesus Christ, the glorious Father, may give you the Spirit of wisdom and revelation, so that you may know him better. I pray also that the eyes of your heart may be enlightened in order that you may know the hope to which he has called you, the riches of his glorious inheritance in the saints.
Eph. 1:17-18 NIV

I didn't want to escape this glorious presence I experienced on that memorable winter day. Not able to utter a word, I was truly like David when he said, "You have made known to me the path of life; you will fill me with joy in your presence, with eternal pleasures at your right hand" (Ps. 16:11 NIV). Just as joy was part of this experience, there was also a reverent fear and trembling. I knew the Lord had taken me captive in an awesome way. Though there was no escaping, I wasn't quite sure why.

Beginning to know the Holy Spirit had enveloped me and filled the room as a cloud, I scarcely understood the vastness of the moment. I prayed aloud, "Lord, you must have something amazing to say to me. Help me to discern it. Help me to get it, Lord, all of it!" At moments, I was sure that my daughter would hear my prayers and sobbing and come running. She never did.

Overcome with tears, it's as if the Spirit had plunged my soul deep in a well and pulled it back up drenched, splashing water everywhere. I pushed back my Bible and workbook to rest my head. "Lord, I have no idea what you are trying to speak to me, but I want to get it so badly because I know you mean for me to. Lord, help me to understand." Surely expecting this Presence to be gone in a flash, it remained long enough to allow some understanding, but not be totally taken away by it. When was the last time you prayed for understanding from the Lord? Take time now to review Eph. 1:17-18 (NIV) on page 46. I encourage you to turn this scripture into a personal prayer, read it aloud every day until its words are etched on your heart. I'm convinced that we need understanding as much as we need anything to survive this earthly journey.

Trying desperately to be calm and collected, I was undone. After reading John 21 and the intimate experience of His Presence, I understood (at least in part) what the Lord was asking, "Are you *my* friend, Mel Ann?"

Responding through tears, "Lord, me? Be *your* friend? You have saved me from the pit. You have bailed me out and given me so many new starts. Of course, you are *my* friend. I have poured out my troubles to you. You have lifted me up and encouraged me. You have been my friend, but how can I possibly benefit you as a friend?"

While we continued the dialogue, the Lord listened. His Spirit was right with me. Reasoning with Him that Peter would be a better friend, I offered a host of other options for the Lord. He would be more pleased with Billy Graham, Henry Blackaby, pastors, missionaries, but not me.

After pouring my heart out to convince Him that He already had better friends than I would be, the question remained, "Are you *my* friend?" He called my name that day in a way and for a purpose that was not only fresh but way beyond me. He spoke through His Word so personally. If you have heard the Lord calling you, how have you responded? Yes, you.

Listen Up, Look Up

As Jesus walked beside the Sea of Galilee, he saw Simon and his brother Andrew casting a net into the lake, for they were fishermen. "Come, follow me,"....
Mark 1:16-17a NIV

In this walk of faith, we are wise to listen and look expectantly. If we learn anything from experiencing God's presence, we learn not to miss what He's saying to us.

The Mobile Register article is dated December 17, 1960. The Heading: *Area Couple Aids in Establishing English-Speaking Church in Mendoza.* Quoting excerpts from the article:

It seems that (Mr. and Mrs.) Britton were sent by the oil industry for which he is employed as a petroleum engineer, to Mendoza, Argentina, where he was soon joined by his wife, Jimmye. There the devoted couple used their opportunity to witness for God and to help the missionaries in Mendoza with their Christian work.

The church, the only English-speaking one in Mendoza, was established in April, 1959, with 15 charter members. The members met in the home of Mr. and Mrs. Britton for the first six weeks.

Now, a regular church building is under construction. This building will seat 200 people and will have Sunday school facilities and a pastor's home. This church, the First Baptist Church of Lujan, has grown from 15 charter members to 40 members.

Mr. and Mrs. Britton explained that they did not know what facilities they would find available when they arrived in Argentina, but they thought that it was God's will that they go there. They found their work and many experiences very inspirational, and it is without a doubt that their presence will be missed in the beautiful South American country.[7]

Mom and Dad answered the call. Somehow they knew it was "God's will that they go there." Answering the call doesn't always mean going to places outside your country or surrendering your life as an international missionary. As lay missionaries during their years in Argentina, their call was to serve and support those who were already serving in missions. Perhaps your call is to serve and support your pastor and church staff or to disciple others in your workplace or church. The Lord prepares you for what He calls you to do. If you don't know, rest assured He desires you to be "on mission" and soon.

I had saved the article for years, and my friends encouraged me to research the status of the church today. My sister and I searched the Internet and soon discovered some results that prove the work God called our parents to do was worth it. The First Baptist Church of Lujan's history records specifically show the church was started by North Americans who had come to work in the oil industry, but had to leave before the church building was complete. These North Americans allowed services to be conducted in their home for the small congregation. Now approaching 700 members, it also has a biblical school and training center that prepares brothers in the faith. Thanks to God for the great things He has done!

6-A—Mobile Register Saturday, December 17, 1960

Area Couple Aids In Establishing English-Speaking Church In Mendoza

MOBILIAN IN MENDOZA
Walter Britton Jr. reads the Church Covenant to the congregation of the First Baptist Church of Lujan in Mendoza, Argentina. He and his wife (insets) aided missionaries in Mendoza in establishing the first English-speaking church.

The Lord has been calling people from Genesis until today. He will continue to call us. He called Adam in Genesis 3:9 and received no answer. He was afraid and naked. When God calls, we do best to bow down, confess our sin and come to Him. Mark 1:16-20 tells us about four fishermen whom Jesus called too. They did not delay.

They dropped everything they had worked hard to acquire and followed Him.

When God calls, it may not be loud, but it will be clear. It may not make sense to you. He summoned Paul by striking him blind for three days. He compelled the disciples through Christ's voice as well. He called out to others in a gentle whisper. The One who calls you is faithful, and He will do it (I Thessalonians 5:24). He will provide a way for you to answer the call. Without warning and almost immediately, feelings of inadequacy and unworthiness can keep us from obedience when God has clearly spoken. In Galatians 5:7-8 NIV, Paul writes under the inspiration of the Spirit about the race we run in the faith:

"You were running a good race. Who cut in on you and kept you from obeying the truth? That kind of persuasion does not come from the one who calls you."

We cannot make ourselves ready enough to be called. Only Christ can transform us. It's in our obedience that *He* will do it. I'd like to ask you to remember a time when the Lord called you to be obedient. What things came to mind immediately as reasons you could not obey?

If you were obedient in spite of the obstacles, keep pressing on! It will be easier to obey the next time. If you struggle to obey, ask the Lord to help you. Take a look at II Corinthians 10:4-5 to see that the power to obey is available. The mind is a battlefield, but the Lord is on our side! He has the power to take thoughts captive that do not align with His. Be careful. The arguments will be suited to your flesh. *But what about your family? Your spouse? What will people think?* The arguments will always threaten what you count dear in life from the most noble, innocent perspective. Remember, this kind of persuasion is not coming from the One who calls you.

One More Call

I want to share one more call. We have supported a dear friend who has been in missionary service for 30+ years in Guatemala. One of Danny Lafferty's monthly newsletters included this:

> Twenty-three years ago this month after having been a pastor for six years and an evangelist for three, I made my first trip out of the United States to the beautiful country of Guatemala. The airfare for that trip was $190 including all departure and airport taxes, but I still had to borrow the money to go. God blessed my life and touched my heart for that country. Even after more than 200 trips and 23 years, I have a deeper burden and love for the precious people there. There is not enough money on this planet to buy the experiences I have had there and the glory of God I have witnessed. The trip earlier this month was no exception.

One more answered the call. In that issue alone, he reported 2,000 people were treated for physical problems, 500 families (approximately 3,000 people) received food, health supplies, and the message of salvation. "We personally prayed with more than 160 precious souls to receive Christ as their Savior. Only God and eternity will tell how many others read the tracts and Bibles and later accepted our Lord."[8] Danny's work there glorifies God, from providing for basic needs to praying with people to receive Christ. It is a work that could not be done without the compelling call and power of the Holy Spirit to obey.

Back to the personal story I began. A mighty wind blew through my life that mild winter day and left me weak from the force of it. I dedicated myself to understanding what had happened and why. The Lord allowed such a blessing, such an intimate calling. He's been teaching me ever since as I have excavated these treasures from the Word. As we dig, we are apprentices under the Master Archeologist. How we can read the Scriptures and understand even a part of them is nothing short of the Holy Spirit's work. The pages of my Bible seem to call me back time and again to the same places with shovel to dig for treasures yet unearthed. The Apostle Paul's prayer becomes mine, and what I am praying for you, "With this in mind, we constantly pray for you, that our God may count you worthy of his calling, and that by his power he may fulfill every good purpose of yours and every act prompted by your faith (II Thessalonians 1:11 NIV)."

As a Christian, allow God to count you worthy of your calling. It's in the smallest acts of faith and obedience that we find and know His purposes for us. Only through the shed blood of Christ are we made worthy. While you are at it, recount what the Lord has taught you, and disclose to Him your desires and intentions.

The Journey Back Down

Still other seed fell on good soil, where it produced a crop – a hundred, sixty or thirty times what was sown. He who has ears, let him hear. Matthew 13:8-9 NIV

I thought I'd never tell what happened on that day. The Lord dealt mightily with me. It was supernatural and would be hard to explain. But I couldn't help it. We must be careful, because the desire to tell all can be a dangerous character flaw. Thank you, Lord, that you can turn our weakness into strength for your glory. I couldn't keep this experience to myself, and I know now He never intended that. By the end of the day, two of my closest friends knew.

I'd like to share with you some notes I recorded in the front of my workbook on that day, and in the margins of those pages of study. I penned these thoughts immediately following this most humbling encounter I'd ever had with my Savior and Lord.

2/20/04 – Peter's commissioning service becomes mine! Lord, I want to serve you! John 21: Becoming a friend of Jesus. Not only is He my friend, but I am becoming His. Friendship, as I know it:

- *Feeling the pain, hurt or other feelings of a friend's heart.*
- *Believing (James 2:23).*
- *Helping the friend with tasks and responsibilities.*
- *Helping bear the burden of work to be done.*
- *Listening to the friend who is speaking.*
- *Talking to the friend who is listening.*
- *Giving help in time of need.*
- *Seeing the need.*
- *Sharing.*
- *Loving.*
- *Giving.*

One of the most important things we can ever do is record our personal encounters with a living, breathing Savior. Why? In Matthew 13:18-23, we read what can happen after we receive the Word into our hearts. As we attempt to understand what God has revealed to us, many other distractions can prevent us from being completely transformed by the revelation. Distractions can result in a walking dead faith. For one, the enemy who is Satan can and will snatch the truth and displace it with doubt and deception. Worries and troubles can so usurp our thoughts that they can seem to attach to our very personhood. The abundance of life can be a blessing, but is often a curse making the revelation unfruitful in us. Read the passage for yourself.

    I never imagined the course of events over the next few days. After such a huge encounter, the enemy of my soul tried to snatch by the roots what the Lord had planted. God allowed me to be aware of two things: 1) you are being sifted as wheat; and 2) you need sifting (see Luke 22:31-32). Christ allowed Peter's life to teach me, and now He was allowing it again. He further sanctified me during that time. Mercifully, He even sent friends to comfort me. Had I not recognized their faces, I'd have thought they were angels because they had no idea what I was going through. What's more, they were not frequent guests in my home. He gave me peace, and I bowed to my Gentle Teacher. Allow the Master Teacher to guide you into the truth of life, even when it hurts. Next, we'll see how Nehemiah responded to a call God placed in his heart.

Present in Time of Trouble

God is our refuge and strength, an ever-present help in trouble. Ps. 64:1 NIV

    Do you remember roll call in grade school? When I entered college, I was pleased to discover that most professors did not keep roll. But just because I was not being called and counted did not negate the need to be present. The professors knew that all too well. You snooze; you lose. You miss much when you miss class.

    Let's look at the life of one man who was present, called, and accountable. He received the call of heaven and made adjustments to answer. Nehemiah was a cupbearer to the king. That meant he tasted from the king's cup to be sure it was not tainted with poison - risky job. But his current position would not be huge in light of what God placed in his heart for the future.

Nehemiah 1:1-4 sets the stage. Two groups of exiles had already returned to Jerusalem over the last 100 years. Nehemiah was not in either group. Some men from Judah were in Nehemiah's presence, and he questioned them about the Jewish remnant and Jerusalem.

Nehemiah mourned, fasted, and prayed for several days about the ruins of the city. Surely concerned, he had no inkling of what to do. The task was great and the burden heavy. When he heard the news of the broken walls of the city, he sat down and wept. Nehemiah was mourning because rebuilding had not begun.

Nehemiah was **present** to recognize the problem.

Sometimes when we hear the kind of news Nehemiah heard, we can *show* concern but never feel it. He was fully engaged and truly burdened about the situation.

Something clearly happened as a result of Nehemiah's tears, mourning, prayers, and fasting. In Psalm 46:1, God is heralded as a present help in time of trouble. Shouldn't we, as His ambassadors on earth, be too?

In this passage, the word *present* means to come forth, appear, meet, be present, find, catch, certainty, deliver, be enough, be here, serve, ready, suffice, and take hold on.[9] If we are becoming like Christ, we are truly present during times of trouble in our circles of influence. I've watched the life of one of my mentors for more than a decade now, though we didn't develop a friendship until recent years. Because we share intimate friendship, I know stuff about her! We talk about the good things God is doing in our lives with great freedom.

During a Sunday morning service at her church, the members had prayed for a family whose mother was on death's bed. Back at home, she was impressed to visit the family in a hospital an hour away, though she doesn't often do hospital visitation. The Lord kept it so heavy on her mind through lunch and cleaning up that she knew she must obey. After she arrived, she understood why.

During the day, the children of this precious mother had come to grips with the decision to remove life support, all except one. She was struggling with the finality of death and hoped her mother's condition would improve. At one point, a family member requested this daughter be left alone for a while without any pleadings to sway her decision. Only my friend and a pastor would stay with her in the hospital's chapel. The daughter struggled with a decision of life or death, while the other two prayed. A quiet peace filled the chapel. She finally decided to let her mother go. As my friend relates, "I felt peace in that place and saw the countenance of her face change." They knew that the very present help in time of trouble had come. How have you most readily been present in times of trouble? Next, we'll look closer at Nehemiah to see how he was not only present, but also called and accountable.

Called and Accountable

Give your servant success today by granting him favor in the presence of this man. I was a cupbearer to the king.
Nehemiah 1:11b NIV

Just like Nehemiah, we can engage and be concerned enough to mourn, fast, pray, help, serve, listen, cook, fill in, clean, sit or babysit, drive, love, or hug. The list goes on.

It would overwhelm us to act on every need. However, when we pray, God will place concern in our hearts for the presence He wants to have through our lives. Not only was Nehemiah present in concern, he was also present in position. We'll see that this gave him credibility and favor to approach the king.

Let's dissect his prayer recorded in Nehemiah 1:5-11. Grab a scalpel and slice it up yourself. To assist, a single word defines each of the four elements of Nehemiah's prayer in this set of verses. Praise (Neh. 1:5); Confession (Neh. 1:6-7); Remind (Neh. 1:8-10); and Request (Neh. 1:10-11).

Do you have a routine way of praying that includes similar portions? If not, consider following Nehemiah's example for a week. When we praise, confess, remind, and request, He'll be pleased with our reverence and submission. Though it might seem Nehemiah was the one doing the calling, Neh. 2:12 reveals that he understood God had initiated the call. He writes, "I had not told anyone what my God had put in my heart to do."

Nehemiah knew who had **called** him.

Make no mistake who initiates the call. We can be terribly weak when it comes to discerning what God has called us to do. So many times, we dismiss or discount something the Lord has impressed on us. We will never get away from the call to obey completely, even if we never do it. Has the Spirit ever compelled you to some deed or speak a word, but you were more convinced that your own flesh was the initiator? Not only was Nehemiah present, he was also called by the Lord, and he would ultimately follow through. Let's look at Nehemiah's accountability to God in what he had been called to do. It's a big word, with big responsibility.

Best we can tell, Nehemiah was sure of what the Lord had placed in his heart. He devised a detailed plan for the rebuilding of the walls of Jerusalem. In Nehemiah 2, we see a myriad of issues he faced in light of this accountability.

Nehemiah was accountable in spite of several obstacles.

Nehemiah was accountable in spite of intense fear (Neh. 2:2b), deadlines (Neh. 2:6), and the opposition from enemy forces (Neh. 2:10 and 4:1). Whether we like it or not, we do not get to use issues or excuses as justification for disobedience. If we truly believe God, we will stand present, called and accountable regardless of the issues we face. Issues are no big deal to our awesome God. It stuns me - the assurance Nehemiah had to move forward. We, too, can know with unwavering confidence, and that can drive us to the end result of obedience. Ask the Lord to give you full assurance of His calling for your *today* and for your *tomorrows*.

5
Sojourners in Friendship

Hold up one hand. Can you count your dearest friends on it? If so, you are indeed blessed. We could discuss friendship for hours. We could debate and tell stories about true friends. Then, we could summarize by listing the qualities we value in a friend. But, most of the time the focus turns inward. What kind of friend do *I* want? Who has been a true friend to *me*? We would lavish praise on those who have been *our* friends. But what qualities in us are pleasing to the Lord regarding our relationships?

True friends are hard to find. My husband and I have discussed how it is even more difficult after marriage than before. Life gets so busy, and the time to develop new relationships is not easy to find. So, what is friendship? Poems and quotes are eye-opening. Efforts to define friendship can be revealing, but let's gaze at the gospel on the matter. There's nothing like the biblical perspective. It's the only truth onto which you and I can place our grip.

What about you and me? What kind of friend are you? What kind of friend am I? In the next few chapters, we'll discover what God expects of us in friendships and other similar relationships. When we take the focus off what *we* need and look through different lenses, we'll see the priorities in a new light. What are others searching for in a true friend? That's a good question. What does the Lord desire from us?

Friendship and Relationship Freedom

Who can discern his errors? Forgive my hidden faults.
Keep your servant also from willful sins;
may they not rule over me. Psalm 19:12-13a NIV

Let's treat friendship like a road trip on a freeway of sorts, with you and me as sojourners along the road. For friendship to flourish, we've got to roll a few rocks out of the path to travel more freely. Early in the pages of scripture, we see the frustrations of relationship between Isaac and Abimelech (see Genesis 26:12-16). We have all dealt with this at one time or another. Our sinful nature, along with our enemy's taunting, makes the green-eyed monster of jealousy come alive. We must move jealousy and envy out of the path before we can begin to see freedom in our friendships. This internal monster will eat us alive, and make us miserable in the process. When the monster is full grown, it can no longer hide inside of us, but jealousy will rear its ugly head in words and deeds.

Another place that we see some obstacles which could damage a relationship is in Genesis 29. Laban, in an effort to gain a son-in-law uses deception, manipulation, selfish ambition, and control. When we try to control others to our benefit, we create huge stumbling blocks that must go. Not only will we enslave our relationships, they probably won't last long.

The acts of our sinful nature are ones we hate to admit or even mention, but they can also be devastating to a relationship: things like sexual immorality, impurity, promiscuity, idolatry and witchcraft, hatred, discord, jealousy, fits of rage, selfish ambition, dissensions, orgies and the like (Galatians 5:19-21 *NIV*). Some of these are offensive to even put in print, but they should be brought to light with regard to relationships.

I've learned many hard lessons about selfish ambition in regard to relationships. *I* must go. *Me* must be moved out of the way. That's the bottom line. We can call it what we want to, make it sound better, and justify it. But it is an act of the sinful nature, and is the way of the world around us. An obvious truth, I know, but how often are we drawn to the way of the culture in which we live? Ask the

Lord now (in writing) to reveal any act of the sinful nature in your life. On an index card, record Psalm 19:12-13 previously noted and prayed by David many years ago. Begin to pray this once a day.

Only the Lord can discern and reveal the errors in our lives that are now hidden. Pride is like a cave into which we crawl and hide from the other sins in our lives. It was for Satan, so we should look for it in our lives. You know about fault lines in the earth's surface now, but we don't know when they will turn into gaping holes. Pride is a hidden fault that threatens our relationships with others, and ultimately with God. If you sincerely want the Lord to reveal and forgive your hidden faults, He'll do it. Many times, they are things in our lives so obvious to others and only hidden from us. I'm sure we'd search longer and find other "stumbling rocks" in our path, but none bigger than jealousy, selfish ambition, and pride.

Are you the first to speak to someone you know, or don't know?... Hold a door for someone or let a car into traffic ahead of you?... Or smile and make eye contact with passersby?... Some people are more outwardly friendly than others. These may be some outward expressions of friendliness, but the real thing is much deeper. It's ironic. Sometimes initially friendly people have placed a guard past which point no one can go. Others you'd never expect from their outward display of interest become dear friends.

Strong's Exhaustive Concordance reveals 107 references on friendship in God's Word. There are two major definitions, plus a few less referenced meanings. About one-fourth of the references are in Psalms and Proverbs. Let's review the definitions:

In Hebrew, friend *reya* is an associate (more or less close), brother, companion, fellow, friend, husband, lover, neighbor.[10] A lesser known definition of friend *ahab* denotes affection (sexual or otherwise) in the definition as in to be beloved or liked.[11] The word *alluph* as friend is only referred to twice (Proverbs 16:28 and 17:9), though its meaning is worth noting: familiar, a friend, also gentle; hence, a bullock (as being tame; applied although masculine to a cow), and so, a chieftain (as notable, like neat cattle), captain, duke, governor, (chief) friend, guide, ox.[12] Finally, in Greek, *philos* is friend, fondly, friendly (still as a noun), an associate, neighbor.[13]

If the Lord has revealed more "stumbling rocks" to you that would put you flat on your face in the path of friendship, search the Scriptures to learn more. You will not be led astray.

Warning Signs

But I am afraid that just as Eve was deceived by the serpent's cunning, your minds may somehow be led astray from your sincere and pure devotion to Christ.
II Cor. 11:3 NIV

We'll unearth a few stories to help us understand ourselves and others in regard to building friendships and other relationships, and the great need to be careful the distance we travel when there are "issues". Do you have friendships with "issues"? By issues, I mean that it seems there are always some sensitivities involved. Perhaps you can see their faces now. A few stories can make clear the need to be cautious about the distance we travel for a friend.

Gary and I spent our honeymoon in beautiful Steamboat Springs, Colorado. The snow was like white dust, and the base was perfect for skiing. It may have been as light as dust, but it settles on the roads like thick white fleece blankets. Gary had never driven in wintry climates. As Dad would say, "he was as nervous as a long-tailed cat in a room full of rockers!" With a new bride and a rented

SUV, driving in this kind of weather was almost more than my new husband could stand.

He navigated nicely until Rabbit Ears Pass. The name fits the lay of the road well. Warning signs were posted everywhere. Winding roads. Steep inclines. Low shoulders. If not for poles on the roadsides, we wouldn't have known where the pavement stopped and the snow-covered banks dropped sharply. It was quite a journey. We passed through the rabbit ears safely, thanks to cautious driving by my new groom.

Let's ponder some warning signs in friendship before we move on to the more scenic view. We'll see that friendship's freeway has necessary speed limits, road blocks, and caution signs we must heed. In Deuteronomy 13, the Israelites were commanded to put to death anyone who enticed them away from sincere devotion to the One True God.

Thank goodness this does not apply directly to us since we no longer live under the law, but grace! Friendship must still be guarded and regarded sincerely so that we are not led astray to worship anyone or anything other than the One True God. Under grace, Paul encourages us not to easily put up with those who attempt to lead us away from sincere and pure devotion to God (II Cor. 11:3-4). Guarding our hearts in friendship is one warning sign we want to heed.

One who entices is better a distant acquaintance than a close friend.

In II Samuel 13, we read that Amnon's friend, Jonadab, devised a plan to help Amnon rape his own sister, Tamar. Amnon was King David's son. The descriptive term used for this friend in the passage is shrewd or subtle. It has in its root meaning the word "wise". In this passage, however, it means wise in a cunning kind of way.[14] The result of Jonadab's scheming was terribly destructive. We can't scheme to get what we want. Selfish ambition is rampant here, don't you think? It may have been Jonadab's scheme, but Amnon was no innocent bystander. He knew Jonadab's shrewdness, and still Amnon called him friend. This incident set the stage for major heartache and conflict in David's family line. Tamar was never "righted" on this earth, but that's another story. The Lord says, "Vengeance is mine" (Romans 12:19).

David did a good bit of scheming himself. Sadly, his son turned out to be like him in many ways. The same kind of generational behavior can happen in any family line, royal or not. We want to learn what true friendship is. We must become what we want our spiritual and physical children to be: True Friends of Jesus Christ.

One who schemes does not have our best interest at heart.

Job is an Old Testament great from whom we can learn about suffering more by the help of his friends than if he'd had none at all. His friends came to console (Job 2:11), but their "helpful" words actually hurt him to the core.

Let's turn now to another passage and take a close look at how *not* to be a friend by summarizing what both the Lord and Job said about his friends.

A man in despair should have the devotion of his friends. (Job 6:14)

Never trade your friend for something else of value. (Job 6:27)

Never forget your friends. (Job 19:14)

Have pity on your friend when tragedy strikes. (Job 19:21)

God is angered when we condemn and judge. (Job 32:3)

God is angered when we speak wrongly on His behalf. (Job 42:7)

God will hear us when we pray for our friends. (Job 42:10)

It's best to be one of fewer words when a friend is hurting or mourning. Listening is always better. It's even alright to ask open-ended questions like: How do you feel? What questions do you have? What can I do to help? What do you need right now? Why bad things happen is hard to explain or understand, and it's not our place as friends to try. It's not our place to speculate either. God calls us to be there for a friend in prayer, heart, and spirit. Our tongue has the power of not only life, but death (Proverbs 18:21).

One who judges or condemns leaves a wake of suffering in others.

As soon as I received news that one of my college roommates had been diagnosed with breast cancer, I began to pray. I am praying not only for her, but also that the Lord would direct me each time I have an opportunity to talk with her. Interceding in prayer is the most effective way I can serve her. Each time we have spoken since Kathy began treatment has been special not because of anything I have said, but because we have prayed together.

Now that we've taken heed to the warning signs, let's draw attention to some "rules of the road" on this friendship journey. Remember these warning signs. You will surely encounter some of them again from the pages of God's Word on your journey.

Rules of the Road

The pleasantness of one's friend springs from his earnest counsel. Proverbs 27:9 NIV

Remembering that most Scripture references on friendship are concentrated in Proverbs, you may have figured we would eventually visit some of those stops on the road. We've referred to friendship as a pathway or freeway as we rolled some stumbling rocks out of the path to travel more freely. Even with those rolled aside and the path clear, there are a few more things that make friendship a road of freedom. Without some guidelines from the Word, I'm headed straight for the potholes. Let's consider some **"Rules of the Road"** for friendship:

Rule #1: Be careful what you promise to a friend. (Proverbs 6:1-3 and 17:18)

Rule #2: Don't choose your friends based on their financial status. (Prov. 14:20-21)

Rule #3: Do not gossip. (Prov. 16:28)

Rule #4: Overlook an offense. (Prov. 17:9)

Rule #5: Let love rule in your heart. (Prov. 17:17)

Rule #6: A few close friends are better than many acquaintances. (Prov. 18:24)

Rule #7: Don't choose your friends based on their influence. (Prov. 19:4 and 6-7)

Rule #8: Let your heart be pure; let your speech be gracious. (Prov. 22:11)

Rule #9: Listen to friends who are honest with you. (Prov. 27:6)

Rule #10: Be sincere when you give counsel to your friends. (Prov. 27:9)

Rule #11: Accept the sharpening iron of a friend. (Prov. 27:17)

Of these friendship "rules of the road", which ones impact you the most?

In these rules, we see some commonalities: speech, love, and wealth (or the lack thereof). When speech is motivated by the sinful nature within, it will be loaded with hints of bitter envy, selfish ambition, earthly concerns and desires, unspiritual thoughts and ideas, disorder and evil. However, when the words on our tongue are motivated by the Holy Spirit, they are full of wisdom, mercy, love, peace, consideration for others, submission, sincerity, impartiality, and righteousness.[15]

The "Rules of the Road" for friendship are best guided by Scripture. When we read Proverbs, it's easy to zone in on mankind's pitfalls through the ages. As imperfect as we are, we all need friendship.

I was in a small group discussion recently where the facilitator asked a thought provoking question we were to answer individually, if we could. The question was, "What truly satisfies you?" There were those who struggled to answer the question at all. Others knew it was family, and even one answered that the Lord Jesus was her satisfaction. There's an answer that still stands out from a wife and mother with three children. She meant no harm in saying it, but it jogged something in me. She said (and I paraphrase) that she is most satisfied when she is all alone in her home with no one around for whom to care or worry. There *is* something good about solitude. We all need it, and I often look forward to my own opportunities for it.

With the exception of interaction with our families, we could so orchestrate our lives not to involve or influence others unless absolutely necessary. We'd have our own perfect solitude without any need in ourselves to reach out and connect in relationships. Rick Warren's *Purpose Driven® Life* poses this challenge, "At some point in your life you must decide whether you want to *impress* people or *influence* people. You can impress them from a distance, but you must get close to influence them, and when you do that, they will be able to see your flaws. That's okay."[16]

We never know who God intends for us to befriend. The rules we have referenced from the wisdom of Scripture help us see friendship from a biblical view. He is helping me to see others through His eyes.

One in Spirit

After David had finished talking with Saul, Jonathan became one in spirit with David,
and he loved him as himself. I Sam. 18:1 NIV

One of the most renowned Bible stories about friendship is that of Jonathan and David. We can learn from it as we travel the road of friendship together. Jonathan loved David as much as he loved his own life. So much so that he made a covenant with David and gave him the clothes off his back and some vital weapons for battle. They both would later learn just how badly he needed the weapons of warfare.

Because the story of Jonathan and David is sordid and full of drama, please read it for yourself in I Samuel 18-20. Jonathan put his life in danger for the sake of his friend. Covenants were hugely important in those days, and still should be. Because these men had a covenant, Jonathan ensured that David's life would be spared, if even at the expense of his own.

Have you had a friend who seemed to disappear as quickly as he or she appeared? I sure have, but she'll always be my friend. That's where David and Jonathan were. They had a covenant, but circumstances necessitated separation for reasons too many to list. One stands out in particular: Jonathan's father wanted David dead!

See one critical scene in this friendship before we also part ways with it. In the midst of fearful circumstances and certain death (I Sam. 23:15-18), Jonathan helped David find strength in God. He told David not to be afraid. He said, "My father Saul will not lay a hand on you. You will be king over Israel, and I will be second to you. Even my father Saul knows this." At that moment the two of them made a covenant.

If I didn't have the encouragement of my friends, my faith would falter. I wouldn't treasure those friends like I do. Again, the two men made a covenant. This time, Scripture doesn't show whether or how they marked it. But to mark the first covenant, Jonathan gave David practically all he was wearing and his weapons.

The Lord overlaps lives in His perfect timing. We shouldn't be surprised that parting is often a slice of God's purpose. More than a decade ago, the Lord placed us in a different church. We didn't know a soul, but quickly connected with the pastor and his wife. We'd been in their home, and they'd visited ours. Mark and Mary Byrd (and their girls) are a precious family. The Lord strongly impressed to me: "Don't you dare put them on a pedestal!" I suppose I'd been guilty of such in the past.

Not much time had passed before the Lord spoke to me about our relationship: "Befriend Mary." That was it.

When the Lord speaks to your heart, do you also find He speaks in short, simple but direct ways?

I said, "Lord, she is a pastor's wife. She's been at this church for more than two years. I'm sure Mary has plenty of friends, maybe even too many." Again, He said, "Befriend Mary." "But Lord, why? They are not surely going to be here forever. Pastors come and go; you move them on." He persisted, "Mel Ann, befriend Mary."

I continued my eloquent debate, reasoning how people probably dump their problems on her far too often, not to mention that a minister's family is in a glass house being watched and judged at all times. Again, He said to me in no uncertain terms, "I'm not asking you to get a new friend for yourself. I'm asking you to be a friend to Mary." Finally, I agreed to obey as much as I possibly could.

Mark and Mary were soon led to another church. It was a sad time, though we've stayed in touch since then as best we can. I still don't understand why, but God does. Perhaps, He wanted me to see what it was like to purposefully befriend someone on this earth so I could know how to befriend Him. I have a mind to believe the purpose was two-fold, and just as meaningful to meet Mary's needs. This couple richly blessed my life and encouraged my family during a treacherous transition. If the Lord calls you to befriend someone, He has reasons. He intends to use you to minister to the needs of another without regard to your own. Thank you for the privilege of friendships, Lord! Pray now and ask God to help you be a friend in a way that is pleasing to Him, and to purify your relationships.

Defining Friends

If you need your fingers and toes
to count your closest friends,
Then maybe your definition of one

is broad, from end to end.

For closest friends come sparingly
as through this life you pass,
Your most dear friends have qualities
that put them in another class.
If a friend once was, but where is she when...
Then that's not a friend on whom you can depend.
Or if a friend sees your faults and quickly turns from you,
Then that's a "friend" who failed to ask,
"What would Jesus do?"

Enough! Enough! - To talk about what a friend is not,
Just focus on those precious traits that really mean a lot.

When you think of her, she's thinking of you...
be very sure of this.
No envy, strife, or guilt is there...
it's not worth the fuss.
For her company, you'd miss.

The road to friendship isn't one way,
There's care and compassion to and fro,
And there's no toll to pay.

The road is big and wide enough for other friendships too,
No jealousy is allowed to cross between the two.

A friend knows what you're thinking,
it seems she reads your mind!
But gives her ear to hear your thoughts,
and dear, sweet time.

Happy when you're happy, sad when you're sad.
A Christian friend intercedes for you
when things look really bad.

Distance doesn't separate
the connection between your lives,
For when you reunite,
it's as if she'd been there all the time.
A true friend is like a home without any walls,
Only doors through which to walk.
That friend's many windows give light to the soul,
And help you find refuge from life's greatest calls.

It doesn't take much effort when friendship first sparks,
But it's a pleasant energy that starts the fire
and keeps it warm
For years and years to come.

For Dear Friends, by Mel Ann Sullivan

From Gap to Glory

> *Then Peter said, "Silver and gold I do not have,*
> *but what I have I give you.*
> *In the name of Jesus Christ of Nazareth, walk."*
> *Acts 3:6 NIV*

      Our last stop on this friendship freeway will be a gap of sorts in the journey of life; one the Lord clearly calls His people to fill. In this story, the Lord was looking for someone to stand in the gap, but He finds no one. It wasn't a literal gap, but more of a symbolic gap. Ezekiel was the man who spoke this word of the Lord to His chosen people in Ezekiel 22. It may seem like a strange place to stop, but the Lord has purpose in applying it to our lives. Read Ezekiel 22:23-31 to prepare for the place we are going. In the latter half of Ezekiel 22, we see that Jerusalem was ravenous for sin from the prophets to the priests to the people.

Count 'em - you see 15 phrases or words that describe the sad and shameful situation. The Lord looked for a man, just one, who would stand in the gap to keep His wrath from raining down on their heads. He found no one. Have you ever felt like you were serving God alone in your circle of influence?

There is hope. God will allow help to come to those who are in need of His love, resources, words, mercy, and grace. But He intends to use you and me to stand in the gap. He will use us in minute and magnificent ways if we allow Him. There are those times when He purposes to use *you* specifically. Have you received a personal call to act specifically for the sake of either one person or a group of people?

I've mentioned a missionary we have supported. I had always read Danny Lafferty's monthly newsletter, but this one was different. He reported about a church planting at Aloetenango, Guatemala. The need totaled $1,483 to purchase cement, sand/gravel mix, plastic chairs, Spanish Bibles, and some roofing material. They needed cement for the floor so that "during the rainy season, water won't flow through the building."[17]

As I read about the need, I wept. The Lord said to my spirit: "The Bibles are yours." I absolutely knew I had to be obedient. I called Danny right away to tell him. My mind was swirling. My brothers and sister had given in the past, and I felt they needed to hear the story. They each committed resources for the gravel, cement, and other items. A dear friend called the next day, and we were catching up since our last visit. As we talked, I told her what the Lord had done in my heart about the Aloetenango church. I had no intentions other than for her to be blessed. Before we ended the call, she asked to help with the Bibles. Together, the five of us were able to send DLEA about $1000. Danny is standing in the gap. We were standing in the gap.

Standing in the gap doesn't always include financial resources. Let's stop at the gate called Beautiful. The Lord anointed Peter to stand in the gap there; bringing immediate results in the life of at least one man (Acts 3:1-10). In this passage, a crippled man asked Peter and John for money. Instead, he received a miracle. But the crippled man gave the disciples something too - his attention. Whose attention do you have?

When we have someone's attention, the Lord has captured it for His purposes. The Lord is at work in you and those around you. My mother-in-law said recently if she had her younger years back, she would have poured more of God's love into her children. She told me that when she was a child she heard more about God's wrath. The love of God was not poured in until years later, so she feared she had not poured it into her children as much as she would have liked. I reminded her that she still pours into her children, grandchildren and great grandchildren. She definitely has their attention and love! In the next chapter, I'll share with you a story of attention-getting proportions.

So, who has your attention in the same way that Peter had captured the crippled man's (Acts 3)? Years ago, I attended a banking conference in Atlanta, Georgia. These conferences are great, because they often allow us some built-in free time. Most were going to the Braves game, but not me. With three younger children at home, I didn't often have this much free time. It's probably better for my personal lifestyle, but where I live allows little opportunity to browse through shops and catch a movie right next door. So that was my plan for evening.

During my quiet time that morning, I shared some of my concerns with the Lord. I knew no one there, had traveled alone, and prayed He would present an opportunity to serve Him on that day. But the morning was all about business, and I was looking forward to an afternoon just for me.

Not long after arriving at the mall, I came to an area under construction. It was not only loud, but quite desolate. I made my way around the escalators, then heard a voice faintly calling, "Mam? Mam?" It was so faint that I could have ignored it and she'd have never known. It would have been hard for anyone to hear. Turning to look back, I realized I had passed by and not noticed her. I looked into her eyes as if to say, "Did you call me?" I walked back to her. She asked if I knew a place she could stay for the night, and I said, "I don't live here or know the area." I asked her if she knew a shelter in the area where she could go. She knew where she could go, but would have to supply her own food and such.

My mind racing, I was fully aware that many homeless make their living in the Atlanta area. When you give them money, it's often used for drugs or alcohol. As she pointed to her cheekbone she said, "I had a fight with the father of the children." She said she had to leave. I saw no sign of a bruise or mark on her cheekbone, and I wondered if she was telling the truth. For all I knew, the guy she was with could have been parked outside waiting for her to return with the goods from her cunning. A total distrust of the situation prevailed in my spirit until the Lord intervened. God does have His way of intervening.

The young lady in that mall was God's divine interruption in my day. He quickly reminded me of my prayer that very morning. Immediately, the three babies were in living color before me. One was less than a year old; the other toddler was trying to climb the railing. The oldest was sitting by her mother on the bench. A long duffel bag stuffed full was forced into the storage area under the stroller. Runny noses needed wiping. Empty bottles needed filling. A family needed help. Those three could have been my three. That mommy could have been this mommy.

The Lord took over. Kneeling to her level, I asked when the children last ate, and a few more questions. She heard about my three children and how close they were in age. I asked if she knew Jesus and whether she knew what it took to get to heaven. I prayed with her. During this time, Acts 3:6 glared before me: "Silver and gold have I none, but such as I have, give I thee" (KJV). Before we parted ways, I parted with my cash (which wasn't much). It would be enough for a meal. Later, at the other end of the mall, the same young mother was strolling her children. It was confusing that I first saw her near the food court. Why was she at this end so soon? I don't know the answer. But my enemy wanted me to think that she was not using the money for food and was still "working the crowd" for more. When our eyes met that time, she asked, "Where is the food court?" I told her, and walked on.

I'll never forget Acts 3:6. We are not responsible for the outcome when we are called to obey. We are only called to obey. One of my co-workers related an incident to me later about a time she was helped by someone who "stood in the gap" for her. She had never seen the lady and has not seen her since, but she said, "Her face will be forever etched in my memory." You are in good company when you help people out of obedience whether or not you think they need or deserve your help. Be warned that you are sure to meet opposition when you become more like Christ and befriend sinners (Matt. 11:18-19). Expect it, but don't be discouraged from what God asks you to do.

The ultimate stand took place in the gap between heaven and earth. Jesus hung on the cross of Calvary suspended between heaven and earth, and touching neither. He was filling a gap that only He could fill. We didn't deserve what He gave, but we needed it more than anything. We deserved death. Nothing else would accomplish the same results to forgive the sins of all mankind. Because He stood in the gap for us, we stand in the gap for Him and others. We can serve the Lord for years, but we never have a right to say we've paid our dues. Stand in the gap until you fall face down in glory, for this is your reasonable service.

6
Abraham, Friend of God

Even before God changed his name, He was summoning Abram to friendship. Why was Abraham considered a friend of God? What so attracted God to this man that He would deliberately call him "Abraham, my friend"? I want to know, don't you? If we can it figure out, perhaps we can pattern our lives in the same way. We'll study significant turning points in Abraham's life, as well as character traits and critical actions. Our time with him will shed light on why God endeared him so intimately during his days on this earth. Imagine learning some simple truths from someone so revered and respected as Abraham. Ah, the treasures hidden in the life of a man who stood in time like a beacon in the ocean. Join me as we travel through his life.

When you review Genesis 12:1-8, it might occur to you that it's nice to have friends in high places! Looks like Abram had the one and only Friend he needed. So do we. Our focus is this: Our Friend in high places calls for friends in the low place of earth to display His glory among the peoples. When you read verse 3, think of God's words (paraphrased) to Abram in this way, "Listen, Abram, any friend of yours is a friend of mine. And about your enemies, I'm watching your back. I've got you covered." That's how we'd say it today. And did He ever fulfill it!

The Friend in High Places

O, our God, did you not drive out the inhabitants of this land before your people Israel and give it forever to the descendants of Abraham your friend?
II Chronicles 20:7 NIV

Abram appears on the horizon of time in Genesis 12. Back in Genesis 11:26, the genealogy of Shem reveals that Terah was the father of Abram. Terah was 70 years old when Abram was born. There's not much recorded about the many listed in Shem's genealogy. Then, there he is - Abram, who later became Abraham. Let's take our time with this friend.

In the first verse of Genesis 12, God gave Abram a direct command, "Leave!" And Abram did. He was immediately obedient. If Abram was not leaving something special and good, it would be an easy thing to do. Have you ever known someone who got married as a means to leave a bad situation at home? I have. It was actually an elopement, but Abram was called to leave a comfortable environment. Abram was commanded to leave his country, his relatives, and even his own father.

One thing of which we want to be sure: Friendship with God is different from any other we can imagine. In Abram's act of obedience, he continually built altars to the Lord (Gen 12:7, 8; 13:4, 18). Friendship with the Lord is never something about which to boast. The Lord abhors a prideful heart. *Wow, I'm a friend of the Lord! What about that?! It's because of my life, my testimony.* NO! Notice as God was establishing intimacy with him, Abram was humbling himself before omnipotent God. When God calls you to friendship, you will be humbled. You will want nothing else but to please Him in all you say and do, not that you will. Friendship with God is not a call to perfection, but a call to honesty and purity as this man's life will reveal.

In Gen. 12:10-20 we see Abram's "left turn" to Egypt. God had clearly told Abram that he was to go to the land that God himself would show him, and that he ultimately did. We see in this passage he makes somewhat of a "left turn" without any indication he sought the Lord, nor did he build an altar to the Lord once he arrived. Have you ever wandered from God's plan because you had not inquired of Him?

Hindsight *can* be 20/20 if we let the Lord use our "left turns" to show us where we "turned left". I have heard Him say to me many times, "Child, this is where you went wrong. It was this (motive, desire, reaction, or action) that landed you in a place where you were out of my will." I'd rather the Lord teach me a lesson than flesh and blood, wouldn't you?

We won't spend much time with Abram in Egypt, but things did not go well there. It seems Abram chose his own way in going to Egypt. Then, he convinced Sarai to deceive the Egyptians. The situation worsened as Abram's faith wavered like a buoy instead of standing like a beacon. Abram was motivated by fear (v. 12-13). Our decisions should not be motivated by fear. Fear does not come from God (II Tim. 1:7), though we are certainly commanded to reverently fear God alone and follow Him by faith.

The Lord allows "left turns" in our lives. He intends to use them for our good. Based on scripture, what Satan intends for evil, the Lord can use for our good. He's faithful to work everything out for His purposes. A look at the times in Scripture God told His children not to be afraid is a Bible study in itself. Satan has no chance for complete victory, try as he may. Momma used to say, "He may win a few battles, but God will win the war."

A Necessary Leave of Absence

The Lord said to Abram after Lot had parted from him, "Lift up your eyes from where you are and look north and south, east and west. All the land that you see I will give to you and your offspring forever.
Genesis 13:14-15 NIV

We see in the beginning of Genesis 13 that Lot (Abram's nephew) went with him. If God had spoken to my uncle and made those kinds of promises, I'd want to follow him too. I'd have wanted to stay under his wing, just like Lot, but we don't know whether he knew about these promises. Relationships can be sticky, especially when they involve blood relatives. Read Genesis 13:1-13.

Abram quickly initiated some resolutions in these verses:

Abram took **initiative** to:
- **dissolve** the conflict.
- **divide** the relatives and possessions.
- **deliver** the best to Lot.

Taking initiative is a hard thing to do. We'd rather wait for others to apologize or admit they were wrong. Sometimes, we're satisfied to sweep the issues under the rug and pretend they do not exist. What's worse, often our idea of taking initiative means this, "I'm going to give her (or him) a piece of my mind!" OR "I'm going to teach him (or her) a lesson." Unless we take initiative in love and are led by the Spirit, we'll be misled altogether. There are a number of indications that Abram handled this quarreling God's way (Matt. 5:23-24; 19:30 and Prov. 11:17). God allowed Abram to finish the "leaving" he started. It was a necessary leave of absence and God's purpose at this time.

In Gen. 13:14-17, it appears that Abram may have questioned whether he should have so quickly laid down his rights for his nephew? He had the authority and seniority. He could have given Lot the least appealing land and possessions. Have you ever been led to lay down your rights and desires and then later questioned your decision? God reassured Abram regarding his actions on Lot's behalf by telling him again to lift up his eyes and look in all directions at the land he would be given (Gen. 13:14-15).

I can almost hear the Lord confirming to Abram (paraphrased), "Hey, you are on the right track. Remember the promise I gave you?" Sometimes we don't verbalize our thoughts on a matter before the Lord immediately knows them and responds to us. That is amazing!

This time, Abram did not ask for confirmation, but the Lord gave it anyway. It's okay to ask. He knows we need it. We'll see later as Abram's relationship with God developed and matured, he began to ask for confirmation. Hasn't God confirmed His plans to you at a time when you may have had questions that certainly needed answers? Thank Him today for directing your path as specifically as you need it.

Did Abram get the short end of the stick? Probably so, in our eyes. That's not all bad since scripture tells us if we humble ourselves, the Lord will exalt us in due time. Abram humbled himself as he built an altar to the Lord (Gen. 13:18). Our next stop in Abram's life will find him as the first responder to a search and rescue operation.

Lot's Plot Thickens

And he blessed Abram, saying "Blessed be Abram by God Most High, Creator of heaven and earth."
Gen. 14:19-20 NIV

Lot's life got complicated after he left his uncle. The story ensues at Genesis 14:1 – 12. By this time, he might have wished he had stayed with old Uncle Abram. With Lot's enemies in hot pursuit, let's see what happens. Abram parted ways with Lot in love and in God's way. God promised to bless those who blessed Abram and curse those who cursed him. We might consider that Lot had cursed Abram by not resolving the conflict and by selecting what appeared as the most and best portion of land.

It's hard to swallow. We'll see another aspect of Abram's character in Gen. 14:14. There's a thing we say in the South when the depth and potential of someone's character is on display. Unfortunately, usually when a negative aspect of character is involved, we say, "I saw her true colors..." or "his true colors came shining through." We can learn from the truly positive colors that shine through Abram in the next scene as he unleashes all his resources to go to Lot's defense.

Christ goes to the Father in our defense (see I John 2:1), just like Abram took Lot's defense. In the King James Version, there is a reference to Jesus as our advocate. An advocate is an intercessor, consoler, and comforter.[18] Abram took Lot's defense in a more literal way with armies and weapons. But Christ's power as an intercessor with the Father is mightier than 10,000 armies. Remember that word - advocate. You've just discovered its only reference in scripture. How does knowing you have an advocate with the Father make you feel when you need defending? Imagine, when we least deserve it (as if we ever do), Jesus is interceding for us. His comfort and peace have come during times of repentance, and I've felt His very real embrace of love, mercy, and grace.

In Gen. 14:17-22, the king of Sodom offered a compromise that Abram knew better than to take since he had sworn an oath. Except in a court of law, we don't talk about oaths much. But it was serious business. According to the King James Version, "he had lifted up his hand to the Lord (v. 22)". That sounds more familiar. It's exactly what political officials do when they are sworn in. That's what oath means. It's something *sworn.*[19] In other words, it's something we promise. We must be careful about making oaths of any kind. When we make an oath, promise to pay a debt, love until death, do a deed, or take responsibility for something, we should do everything possible to stand by it. When we make an oath or a promise, God knows it. Even if it isn't made to God, it is made before Him.

Gary and I had to be careful around our children when they were younger. A promise meant more to them because their understanding of the word hadn't been tainted by the world's way. However, many things can get in the way of fulfilling it. I've heard this from the mouths of so many children (including my own), "But, you promised me!"

Promise something to the Lord today as you pray, if you have a heart to do so. If not, ask Him to give you the kind of heart that allows you to keep promises made.

A Vision for the Future

"But you, O Israel, my servant, Jacob, whom I have chosen, you descendants of Abraham my friend. I took you from the ends of the earth, from its farthest corners I called you. Isaiah 41:8-9 NIV

Abram was waiting. Engagement waits for the wedding. Pregnancy waits for the delivery. And Abram waits for the promise to come true. The impossible dream waits for reality. He could hardly imagine it would come to pass.

As you read Genesis 15:1-20, you'll see that Abram's vision changed his life. The Lord knew he was discouraged. He might have said, "Lord, I know you've made a promise, but I'm seeing no action here." This time, Abram not only voices his frustration, but he also later asks for confirmation.

When we are discouraged, the Lord often reminds us to look up and not around. "Lift up your eyes, child!" He knows if we look around and see no progress, we'll continue in a discouraged state, lose faith, and stop believing what He has told us. In this encounter, we see proof of Abram's strengthened relationship with God.

- Abram was **connected** with God (Gen. 15:1).
- Abram had **conversation** with God regarding his concerns (Gen. 15:2-5).
- Abram then had **courage** to believe God (Gen. 15:6).
- Abram asked for **confirmation** regarding the promise (Gen. 15:8).

Though it's difficult to reason why Abram was endeared by God as a friend, we'll certainly try. By the time we get to Genesis 22, the Lord had changed Abram's name to Abraham. If there ever was a hard test, this one recorded in Genesis 22 would be it. It would compare to Job's loss and Jesus' desert experience.

When the Great I AM calls, "Here am I!" would be an appropriate response. Abraham did not question God, nor ask for confirmation. By now, the intimacy of relationship compelled him to immediate obedience in his hardest test. The Lord asked Abraham to envision his future. It must have appeared foggy from the top of that mountain with Isaac at his side. Next we'll look at how God uses an earthly parallel to show us what He is doing in time and eternity for us. By this, we get a sneak preview of what His plan and purpose looks like on man. God orchestrates a plan working through man who, after all, has been created in His image. It helps us to better understand His ways.

In Genesis 22:5, Abraham's obedience and faith in the willingness to sacrifice his son were acts of worship. Why did Abraham say "*we* will come back to you (emphasis mine)."? Was it that he knew his servants would be fearful if he disclosed why Isaac was going with him? I believe Abraham knew his God would provide the sacrifice, and he envisioned a future that included Isaac. Somehow, he was trusting, even in the testing. Do you find it interesting that he told his servants to stay, but he had to go?

We've come to what any parent would agree is the heartbreaking climax of the story. Genesis 22:9 says that Abraham "bound his son". Bound his son? Bound his son! I suppose by this time Isaac was tied up, literally and emotionally, in knots. Perhaps he was sobbing silently, but still obeying his father. He would have preferred this sacrifice did not include him. Surely, Abraham was just as emotional. Picture the swift throbbing of his heart making its way through his robe. His brow dripped with sweat, while salty tears poured from his eyes. The lump in his throat must have been huge. With the knife in his raised hand, ready to come down on his only son (of promise), the story takes a life-saving turn. Why? Because Abraham feared God. Abraham wasn't the only one. It would be an event Isaac would never forget. An interesting description of Isaac's God is passed down as an heirloom of his heritage when his father, Jacob, refers to God in Gen. 31:24 as the "fear of Isaac".

We underestimate the great value and benefit of fearing God. If we are tempted to look at Almighty God as One only of love, then we miss a very important part of our walk with Him. Oh yes, He is to be feared. This is the only right kind of fear.

Fear or faith? What will it be? The wrong kind of fear freezes us. Faith with a good dose of reverent fear frees us. It's in the Lord's hands. What makes you fearful? Pry open those rigidly frozen fists, and hand your fear over to Him so you can be free to live by faith. Today, let this speak fresh. At this writing, I am anxious and fearful about doing a two-minute video clip to help our staff promote this fall's discipleship training classes. I've tried my best to wiggle out of it, but the Lord speaks to me this morning. Faith frees us when we place our fears in His hands.

From Abraham, with Love

> ..."*and through your offspring all nations on earth will be blessed, because you have obeyed me.*"
> *Gen. 22:18 NIV*

The son through whom the promise of God would come would be at risk in the eyes of the fearful, but not the faithful. Though we've hiked up the mountain with Abraham and his son, let's return to the question for which we seek answers: What so attracted God to Abraham that He would deliberately call him, "Abraham, my friend"?

At times, we will parallel the friendship of God with that of others, but not today. Friendship with God is far different, and it requires great faith and reverence for our Creator as we bow to His purposes alone. Only then will we experience the kind of friendship Abraham enjoyed. Based on the passages listed, we find six important elements of Abraham's relationship with God:

1. Abraham worshipped God. (Gen. 12:7)
2. Abraham called on God. (Gen. 13:4)
3. Abraham believed God. (Gen. 15:6)
4. Abraham feared God. (Gen. 22:12)
5. Abraham did not withhold from God. (Gen. 22:16)
6. Abraham obeyed God. (Gen. 22:18)

One more element might not be quite so obvious: The Lord repeatedly spoke to Abraham (Gen. 12:1), and Abraham listened to His voice. When the Lord speaks to us, it's the one thing we must do to hear him! When we listen intently for the Lord, we will likely hear His voice. Conversely, if we do not hear the Lord speaking to us, chances are good we are not listening.

God speaks in many ways, but He waits for us to listen. Deep down, we may hope He'll speak through great and awesome means. It's more difficult to practice the discipline to listen through His Word, His gentle whisper and His people. If we can't hear Him in the most common ways, He will not likely use more dynamic or emotionally charged means. His desire is always to draw us in really close so that we can hear that gentle whisper and even feel His heartbeat on a matter. I'd like to draw one more conclusion about Abraham:

**Abraham was willing to give God the one part of himself that he loved most –
his son, his only son (of promise), Isaac.**

Has it occurred to you that there is something you may be withholding from God? If you're sure of what that "something" is, the Lord has revealed it to you. Lately, I've given up time, desires, and "must haves". The Lord has finally made it clear that my life is about Christ in me. It's about making His Glory conspicuous, and His Name famous. My circle of influence isn't huge. God has been good to me. He has unchained my captive spirit. I'll be busy making my God famous to my three children, those with whom I work, my church family, other relatives, and anyone else who might see a glimpse of my God in me. He wants the whole heart, but He gladly gives us great reward in return when we are willing to give Him everything in us.

7
Moses, Face to Face

I'd like to see the countenance of Moses' face from the presence of the Lord. Veiled because it was so bright, how long did it take to fade to its original state? I want to know! More than anything, I want to see the heart of Moses, the one who feared God but also feared men, the man who lacked faith and questioned God many times. We see him in Hebrews 11, known as the Hall of Faith. Only time and intimate relationship establish this kind of faith. It takes stumbling in the darkness of doubt and fear, yet obeying when the world crumbles around you. We'll catch a glimpse of Moses' face by way of his heart. If the Lord spoke to Moses face to face as man speaks to a friend, I want to learn why.

The more I study the life of Moses, the more I appreciate his character and walk with the Lord. Abraham and Moses, both spiritual giants, are unique individuals. Thank goodness, we are not cookie-cutter Christians who all respond in the same way, but we are all especially created to respond to God in some way.

To summarize the life of Moses is difficult at best. We'll search for secrets of his relationship as a friend of the Almighty. Unfortunately, we'll bypass some important elements that are not as relevant in our focus on friendship.

A Godly Concern

The Lord spoke to Moses face to face as man speaks to a friend. Exodus 33:11 NIV

Moses' greatest concern was for the treatment of his own people by the Egyptians. Not coincidentally, this was also a concern of God's (Ex. 3:7).

God called Moses to act on behalf of a common concern between them – God's chosen people. When our concerns are common with God's, He's likely preparing us for a future work. According to Psalm 138:8, the Lord will perfect that which concerns us. Amen! His Word says if we delight ourselves also in the Lord, He will give us the desires of our heart (Ps. 37:4).

God was already at work with Moses, whether he realized it or not. Watch out when you become concerned about a situation - truly concerned. It may be the first sign that God intends to use you to help in that very situation. I have a dear friend who deals with an embittered employee every week. My friend tells me she is concerned for the employee's soul and wants her to be free from such sinful, destructive thoughts. This is a great example of the same principle at work in Exodus 2. It could be that God intends to use this friend to help.

We now turn our focus to Exodus 3:1-20 where we find God sharing with His friend intentions to deliver the Israelites and use Moses to accomplish the task. Humility meets fear. Have you ever been asked to do a task that you did not feel adequate to do? If so, how did you initially respond? As we look closely at this situation, we see that a closer look is exactly what Moses desired to do when he saw a bush on fire, but not consumed.

Football rivalries are fierce in our state, especially between the University of Alabama's Crimson Tide and the Auburn Tigers. Gary and I are graduates of the opposing schools. We married to reside in one college town, and then we eventually moved to the other one. People often ask if the old rivalry causes problems on one particular day in college football. I'm not a huge football fan, unless my high school football coach husband is on the sidelines. So, no, it's not a big deal. I worked right across from Auburn University's campus for a number of years. Many football weekends, I watched as the city buzzed with thousands of extra visitors swarming like honey bees. I love my alma mater, but it's hard to get close to the rival fire without getting burned. I'm a silent Auburn fan too. The campus was buzzing, the games were fun, and it was neat to be a part of it all. It's also hard to go to Toomer's Corner after a win without getting toilet paper on you, but that's a different story!

In this situation, Moses got close enough to get burned. But he didn't, nor was the bush consumed. He moved further from thoughts about why the bush was burning and nearer to action by moving closer. As a result, his heart was set afire. When Moses encountered God, he hid his face and was very afraid (Ex. 3:5-6).

In Exodus 3:11 to 4:13, we read that Moses questioned the Lord. It seems more like an interrogation. Let's be careful in our judgment, because we often do the same thing. I interrogated the Lord before ever undertaking the project you now hold in your hands. What emotions often cause us to respond in this way? The Lord used this passage to remind me that even Moses had questions. Though he had many questions, he was still obedient (Ex. 4:3) to do what God asked him to do. Pray now that the Lord will help you be obedient to what He would ask of you, no matter how "small and menial" or "huge and overwhelming" the responsibility.

Tables Turned

"Now go; I will help you speak and will teach you what to say." Exodus 4:12 NIV

Have you ever noticed that life often has a way of serving us what we have dished out? Good or bad, many times "the tables are turned" stands as truth. Today, we take another helping from Moses' life. Pharaoh has been dishing out. Now, it's God's turn to serve.

The Lord showed Moses the miraculous signs He would use in convincing Pharaoh to deliver the Israelites, but look at another great power the Lord used.

"And I will make the Egyptians favorably disposed toward this people, so that when you leave you will not go empty-handed (Ex. 3:21)." We can pray for the Lord's favor! I need the Lord's favor in my home, career, relationships and every facet of life including finances - don't you? We never deserve it, but we can certainly pray for it. Even with the signs and wonders, it would still be necessary to also make the Egyptians favorably disposed toward the Israelites. The signs alone would not be enough. From the middle of Exodus 3 to the beginning verses of Exodus 4, we see a line of questioning by Moses. Then, quite a change in dialogue takes place.

When we, like Moses, move from questioning God to Him questioning us, we might be getting somewhere. The Lord's questions are piercing and often heart-rending. God's questions are intended to settle a matter, while our questions are often intended to argue a matter, or possibly even dismiss it. Though His anger burned against Moses, God still wanted to use Moses and even provided a plan to help him speak. Perhaps this is one of the greatest fears many face – public speaking. But Moses would be speaking for God. When you have daily encounters and opportunities to speak of God's faithfulness and encourage or help someone, be carefully obedient. The Lord will compel you in these moments. He will give you the words to say, and you will simply be His mouthpiece, a vessel through which He chooses to speak. Never underestimate the power of encouraging words, whether spoken or written. In Ex. 4:15b, the Lord told him that He would help him and Aaron speak and would teach them what they were to do.

As far as we can tell, Moses did not tell those closest to him what had happened at the burning bush and the rest of the story (see Ex. 4:18). What if he had? Have you had an encounter with the Lord that you either vowed to tell everyone or absolutely no one? In our encounters with the Lord, it's wise to be mindful that the motive in the telling is pure. At times, we may respond like Moses did in verse 18. He told Jethro (his father-in-law) his plans, but did not tell him all that had happened. At other times, the Lord will speak through us and we'll be able to testify of His faithfulness by telling the details.

Let's unveil some of the relationship this friend shared. Read Exodus 7:1-7, and take note of an interesting statement by God to Moses. Then the Lord said to Moses, "See, I have made you like God to Pharaoh, and your brother Aaron will be your prophet."

We are most effectively used when others see God in us and relate us closely to Him. If they see me more than Him, then we may still have some bowing down to do. The more I bow down, the easier it is for others to see my Father standing over me. To have a servant's heart was John's desire – to be inconspicuous so that Christ would be conspicuous (John 3:30).

Pharaoh began to ask Moses to pray that certain plagues be taken away. Many times, those far from God will ask Christians to pray for them because they believe in our God, His wonders, and our testimony. Moses had compassion and prayed each time Pharaoh asked. He was clear-minded that the reason the prayers were answered is so that he and all the Egyptians would know that "no one is like the Lord our God."

My brother-in-law related part of a sermon that impacted him in a far-reaching way. This preacher suggested that every time we tell someone we'll pray for them and don't we may be taking God's name in vain. It sounds radical, but consider the times you and I promise to pray for someone and later forget. Since that day, my brother-in-law either prays with the person immediately, or he utters a prayer as soon as he leaves their presence. Still today, I hear stories about my mother from those she ministered to in special ways. She often prayed for someone on a moment's notice, wherever they might be, or by phone. I've adopted the same practice, because I know the Lord wants to meet us in our need. If people ask for prayer, they are in need and perhaps their heart is breaking at that very moment. You can hug them and whisper a prayer in their ear. You can send them a scripture in the form of a prayer. With our smart devices, we can even send a voice recording by text! Listen and the Lord will prompt you. Have you ever prayed for someone "on the spot"? If not, what's holding you back?

Our church's Wednesday night service is truly a prayer meeting. Updates are turned in all week, and given to us in writing. Our interim pastor asked some piercing questions recently that cut me like a knife. He asked, "How many of you take this sheet home and place it somewhere you can see it daily and remember to pray over these needs? Or do we trash it on the way out?" When I take it home and place it on the fridge, I will utter a prayer several times each week when I see the list.

When we see answered prayers, it is so Christians and unbelievers will know there is no one like our God. There is comfort in just knowing someone is praying for you. We tend to categorize needs in order of importance, but when *we* have one (great or small), it's extremely important and terribly urgent. You never know what death, sorrow, and suffering is like until it knocks on your door. Have the compassion Moses displayed and pray for those who need it.

A Definite Distinction

But on that day, I will deal differently with the land of Goshen, where my people live; no swarms of flies will be there, so that you will know that I, the Lord, am in this land. Ex. 8:22 NIV

The Lord intends to distinguish between His people and the world. He'll allow that distinction to be obvious in individual lives, family lines, and entire generations. As we continue to walk behind Moses on the trail he blazed, we'll pass through Exodus 8:22-24. Let's look at the first of several times the Lord promises to show favor to His people during the plagues by allowing them to be protected while the plague fell on the Egyptians alone.

For the Lord to show distinction to His children is something I want, what about you? Many times, the prayer of one righteous man or woman brings favor to an entire household, family line, business, and even nation. The favor goes further than that. We are told in Scripture that He will show favor to one thousand generations of those who love Him and keep the commandments (Deut. 5:10).

Moses begged God many times to spare the Hebrew people when God's anger had burned against them. When we pray in alignment with God's will, it will be powerful and effective. As we move through Moses' trail, we find Pharaoh in all his shrewdness. We also unveil another spiritual secret of Moses' life. He was unwilling to compromise (Ex. 8:25-32). Have you ever realized that full obedience is quite difficult when you see a more pleasant compromise? God desired Moses' unwavering obedience. Pharaoh attempted to negotiate a workable plan. Moses' faith in God must have been stout. His reverent, healthy fear of God was a huge factor too.

Often, in relationships, compromise is positive. When Gary and I differ in our opinions and desires, we find it more peaceable to compromise. But when one is not available, I humbly submit to my husband's authority. Even at work, my boss and I openly communicate about best choices and practices. We have a great relationship, so we often come to a compromise even though his authority clearly overrules mine.

Compromise *can* be positive in already healthy relationships. But, it can be unhealthy if we are compromising our faith. It puts us in a position of limited or withheld blessing and favor that otherwise comes with full and complete obedience. Notice another secret about Moses – he spoke the truth to Pharaoh. "Only be sure that the Pharaoh does not act deceitfully (Ex. 8:29)....But I know that you and your officials still do not fear the Lord God (Ex. 9:30)."

It's a wonder Moses was not immediately struck by the guards. When we speak the truth, we must do so as led by the Holy Spirit in love. To hold our tongues when God would have us speak is clearly an act of disobedience. Lord, let us not ever mistake when you would have us to speak on your behalf.

Blueprints Revealed

And when the Israelites saw the great power the Lord displayed against the Egyptians, the people feared the Lord and put their trust in him and in Moses his servant.
Ex. 14:31 NIV

Blueprints can be quite elaborate or entirely basic. A true architect's blueprint places every jot and tittle. Many municipalities require a blueprint before construction begins, but not in our neck of the woods. We didn't have to provide a blueprint to our builder, just some measurements on graph paper. I had the unique duty of walking through my framed home with a black marker to make an X where I wanted every outlet and light switch. As we look at this relationship, notice how God openly revealed His blueprints to Moses. Not only was His plan revealed, but often the purpose behind the plan was revealed. We don't always get to see the entire set of blueprints, but lately I've been losing count of the jots and tittles. What about you? Have you been able to see God at work, *and* some of His blueprints? Ex. 10:1-2 represents many times where the Lord revealed the blueprints to Moses. Be assured that if you are listening to the voice of God, spending time in the Word, and being obedient, He may reveal to you His plan or purposes in your life or the lives of others close to you. Can you think of a personal instance when He has done this? That God is mindful of us is more than a heart can bear, but that we would know at least some of His plan goes beyond my understanding. We don't always get to know everything, but we do get to know some things. Thank you, Lord.

In Ex. 14:31, three results are recorded from the obedience of one man:

1. They feared the Lord.
2. They trusted the Lord.
3. They trusted Moses.

It will turn out like God has planned. His sovereignty is as amazing as His grace. Moses did not believe he could be, nor did he deserve to be, used by God so mightily. Then, he led a frustrated and complaining group of people. Even the Egyptians often received a share of mercy and grace when the plagues were taken from them.

We began with the concern Moses had for the people God would use him to deliver. Now, we'll pay our lasting respects to this man. One day we'll see him in glory, and I have no trouble believing that this time *his* face won't be the only one glowing. For now, I'll share a present day story about how God used the concern of one man to initiate ministry and make His glory conspicuous before many. Sometimes, it's a stretch to apply these Old Testament stories to our lives today, but not this one. Later, we'll look at how God uses the concerns of our hearts to minister to people in need.

    My brother-in-law is passionately aware that he was redeemed from the pit. Not surprisingly, he has a tender heart to the wandering soul, because he so desperately sought the Lord for years before his heart was turned to follow Him. Carroll's job has taken him many miles on interstates across the southeast. He speaks with strangers at virtually every stop along the way. He's not an ordained minister, evangelist or missionary. He's a lay person. He has served his church as a deacon and has played the drums for more than 35 years. But in recent years, he has played them for Jesus.

    He was traveling his normal route down a Louisiana interstate. On this day, he passed a woman walking down the interstate. His heart began to race. He was compelled to stop, but he didn't. With a strong sense that it was the Lord's will, he went back. He went against all logic to obey the stirring in his spirit, as he had a wife and three children at home. Have you ever been compelled to go against all logic to reach out to someone in need? How did you respond?

    When he stopped for her, Carroll immediately called my sister to talk with her. She agreed that he should help and gave her blessing. Whether or not we have a mind to believe it, someone *can* be carrying on life as usual with a good job, happy marriage and healthy children, and end up in a situation like this woman. He listened as they traveled, and she told how drugs and alcohol had messed up her life. By this time, she'd lost her husband, children, home, and her job as a registered nurse. She had no resources and no place to go.

My sister and her husband met some of her basic needs. They paid for clothes, toiletry items, a few meals, and a hotel room. They allowed her to come into their home one day and attend church with them. This situation was not something either of them told anyone. They wanted to help without any commendation or condemnation. Over the next few days, Carroll made arrangements to take her to a Christian rehabilitation home in another city. This required some expense since new residents must provide their own bath and bedding supplies.

Carroll and Janet checked on her a few times, but eventually learned she had left the home voluntarily. Some cronies had lured her back to the lifestyle she'd tried to escape. What a disappointment. Satan would have us believe that any effort to offer someone life-saving hope is a waste of time. It's not true. Carroll obeyed God. After that, it was out of his hands. He was not responsible for the outcome, though he and Janet urged her to stay. One day, each of us will give account for our lives alone, and we'll want to be found faithful to what the Lord called us to do.

My brother-in-law never wanted a soul to know what he had done. A month later, Carroll and Janet's pastor received a letter from one of the volunteer ministers from the Home of Grace. The letter related the story to the pastor at the then First Baptist Church of Hattiesburg, Mississippi. This lady told the volunteer how she came to be a resident there. The volunteer, upon hearing the story, was so moved by the obedience of one man to act on behalf of this wanderer. It's ironic she could not recall Carroll's name, but she remembered the name of the church she attended with them.

The letter was read before thousands at the early service one Sunday morning. The pastor asked the unnamed member that had done this deed to stand, but no one did. He read it again in the second service where Carroll had played the drums during worship and settled into a balcony seat. The entire congregation waited to see who, if anyone, would stand. My sister recalls, "I felt the blood rush to my face and wondered how all this could have happened! I thought, Oh my goodness! He's going to stand up!" His eyes flooded with tears, a heart humbled beyond measure, Carroll rose to his feet. Applause filled the silent sanctuary. It was powerful and moving.

Carroll helped one wanderer, and his God became conspicuous to her and before many. Though he never wanted any glory, he credits Christ in him, the true hope of glory. As you can imagine, Carroll was called upon to serve in ways he never had before. He was ordained a deacon and appointed to head evangelism efforts for his church. He didn't need all the titles to obey God. He was already evangelizing his world, one soul at a time. And he still is. When you are concerned for someone or a group of people, God will use you to minister to them and make His name famous. When was the last time you got personally involved in the life of someone, and it cost you something? Pray today asking the Lord for opportunities to be used in inconspicuous ways to make Him conspicuous.

Last Respects with Lasting Effects

If you are pleased with me, teach me your ways so I may know you and continue to find favor with you. Remember that this nation is your people.
Ex. 33:13 NIV

Consider the obedience of one. We can never foresee the result from our cooperation. We give up unknown blessings when we take obedience lightly. Some of my closest friends and I have been drawn to the issue of obedience for quite a while now. The Lord is requiring it in the smallest daily acts of being a mother, wife, friend, community volunteer, co-worker, church member, and other important positions.

The desire to live a life of obedience must be played out in moments of obedience. Moments make hours. Hours turn into days, and days become years. God is working out what becomes of the years spent obeying Him. We don't usually know the end of the story completely, though He'll give enough of the plot to spur us on to obedience time and again. Moses didn't get to enter the Promised Land, and he pleaded to have that privilege. It wasn't part of the plan, but don't ever forget all that Moses did get to experience. Take time now to discover some of Moses' character traits as seen in Exodus 33.

There are a few not so obvious character traits we want to visit as we come to the end of the trail Moses blazed. Though you may not have seen any of these in Exodus 33, they are worth adding to the ones you discovered.

He was persistent. Ten plagues, and yet Pharaoh's heart was hardened by God time after time. Moses was determined and persistent in spite of the response not only of Pharaoh, but a whole host of people. In what ways do you need to be more determined and persistent?

He was moldable. Moses' first responses to God included questions and excuses (Exodus 3), but the further we journey through his life, the more we see God molding and using him. God can use you from the time you give Him the first excuse to the time He calls you home if you allow Him to mold you. What if God had complete freedom to mold you into His likeness? What would be reshaped first?

He worshipped God. For many years, I have thought of worship as the corporate experience – a gathering of believers who come to a sanctuary at a given time to worship. Scripture does not record that Moses built as many altars as Abraham, though he may have. What *is* recorded repeatedly is that he listened as the Lord spoke (Exodus 15). Moses and the Israelites sang a magnificent song to the Lord. Moses worshipped, and he led others to worship by example.

The Lord is teaching me to have a heart of worship. Worship is what I am doing this very moment – studying God's Word in the preparation of this manuscript. And there are many other ways we worship the Lord outside a literal sanctuary, but inside the sanctuary of our soul.

To pay last respects is always difficult. Moses' trail and the life he led left lasting impressions on me. I was just getting to know him. Let's look back over our shoulders one last time. The Lord himself buried Moses when he died. What kind of friendship is that? Let's remember him alive, holding that rod and standing on the edge of the Nile. Maybe you'd prefer to picture him one last time with Pharaoh declaring the miracles, wonders, and signs of God. The Lord spoke to Moses face to face, as a man speaks to a friend (Ex. 33:11). After all this time we've spent tagging along behind him, let's consider why he had this kind of relationship with his Lord. We've pointed to a few reasons for this special relationship we can actually learn from and mirror in our lives.

Moses was not superhuman! He was just like you and me, stuttering and scared half to death of fear itself, not to mention his own inadequacies. S-S-S-So Wh-Wh-What! We can still be used, and God waits for us to get to the place where Moses found himself before He is able to use us.

Just as God spoke to Moses, His friend, we want God Almighty to speak with us in the same way. Consider some overarching suggestions from Moses' life that we should strive to imitate:

- Pray for your concern to be aligned with God's concern.
- Make sure any humility and fear are rightly related to God.
- Have the glory of God in you to reveal His glory to others.
- Pray for your enemies, and those who believe in your God.
- Be careful not to compromise full obedience.
- Be bold enough to speak the truth in love, and only at the Lord's leading.
- Ask God to trust you with His plans, according to His will.
- Never give up on God's plan.
- Be moldable in the hands of your Lord.
- Worship God in every way.

God positioned Moses so we would learn more about his life than from the Bible stories we may have heard during our childhood. There is more recorded about this man of God than I ever knew, and I encourage you to dig deeper. But we must leave this trail. What a friend God had in Moses. What a friend God wants to have in you, in me. I've recorded Moses' prayer in Exodus 33:13 below with some minor paraphrasing. Take time now to pray it.

Lord, if you are pleased with me, teach me your ways so that I may know you and continue to find favor with you. Remember that I am your child.

8
I No Longer Call You Servant

A Servant's Heart

*You are my friends if you do what I command. I no longer call you servants, because a servant does not know his master's business. Instead, I have called you friends, for everything that I learned from my Father
I have made known to you."
John 15:14-15 NIV*

You have suddenly been transported to 1849. You find yourself in the most beautiful mansion. You're standing at the intricately carved colossal front door holding a cloak. You look around and see servants scurrying like ants attending to the needs of those who reside there. Still trying to gather your thoughts, you glance down to find you are also dressed in servants' clothing. Just then, the master enters the room. Flanked by your co-laborers, one taking his cup of tea while the other places a leather case in his hand, your eyes meet his. As he approaches, you think again about the cloak draping your arm. Immediately, you respond as if its second nature, but you've never been here. Easing the cloak onto the master's shoulders, you notice his eyes have once again met yours. "Now, dear friend, let me share with you my business for today." This scene turns mysterious as you were sure the clothing you wore was that of a servant, not a friend.

True servants of the living God bow in their position, understanding they are so much more in the eyes of a loving Master. Though completely satisfied with the one-dimensional title, a true servant soon discovers he is also endeared as a friend of the Master himself (John 15:14-15). When the Lord directed me to study servanthood, I had no idea what that would entail until I opened my concordance. I kept turning pages to find rows and columns of references (close to 1,000) for servant, servanthood, serve, service, servitude, and tenses of these words. If we can understand and adapt to what it means to be a servant, perhaps we can also be called God's friends. I pray you and I will see this clearly after we take time to bow down and look more closely at what scripture has to say, and that would be A LOT!

    The scripture referenced at the beginning of this chapter, spoken by our Master, has one strong rope attached, and it will anchor us. But it's a mighty big *if*..."if you do what I command". I have been the kind of friend who is here today, gone tomorrow, and back again. Certainly, I wouldn't have been a friend the Lord could count on based on this scripture. I want to become the dependable, consistent friend of my Lord. Servants don't come and go like someone who might help with housework periodically. Servanthood is still a lifetime commitment from God's perspective.

    I'm learning about servanthood firsthand without ever opening my Bible. In past years, summer with three kids and a school teacher for a husband is challenging as time alone is gone after the first child rises each day. I even wondered why the Lord didn't give me this writing assignment during the school year when I could have hours alone to devote to it. I asked Him each night to wake me early enough to have time alone to pray and study before I see more than just *my* sleepy eyes. He was faithful to answer my prayer. As I would lie down, I couldn't wait for morning. But, when it came, I always wanted to roll over and play dead. When I go against my desires and rise anyway, I bow to my role as servant to the Master. I'm beginning to understand.

    In Hebrew, the word servant is *ebed*. This is defined as bondage, bondman, and is from the root word of *abad* which means to work (in any sense); by implication to serve, till, enslave, keep in bondage, compel, do, dress, execute, keep, laboring, bring to pass, be wrought, worshipper.[20]

In Greek, the word servant is *doulos*. This is defined as a slave (literally or figuratively), involuntary or voluntarily, frequently, therefore in a qualified sense of subjection or subservience from root (*deo*) – to bind (literally or figuratively), be in bonds, knit, tie, wind.[21] What is new or interesting to you in these definitions?

Before we search for a true servant in Scripture, let's see what a half-hearted approach might look like. In reading II Kings 10:28-31, you will see that Jehu may be a perfect example of half-hearted servanthood. The Lord held something against him, though he had followed a part of the instructions. God's mercy is great in that He will often allow us to serve, even with half a heart. The commentary regarding this passage in the Life Application Bible states:

> Jehu did much of what the Lord told him, but he did not obey him with all his heart. He had become God's instrument for carrying out justice, but he had not become God's servant. As a result, he only gave lip service to God while permitting the worship of the golden calves. Check the condition of your heart toward God. We can be very active in our work for God and still not give him the heartfelt obedience he deserves.[22]

Even Satan is used as God's instrument. The difference between being an instrument and a servant is at least half a heart.

A Model Servant

In Genesis, we see the blameless example of a servant which many theologians believe to be Eliezer. Not that he was perfect, but his exemplary execution as Abraham's chief servant is a prime model for us to follow. Will you take time now to read Genesis 24? In the first few verses (v. 1-4), Abraham commanded his chief servant to take an oath, and also go and find a wife for his son, Isaac, from among his master's relatives.

We'll look at the specific disciplines this chief servant employed in his daily responsibilities. Eliezer sets a completely human standard for servanthood as we draw a parallel for our lives. He was certainly immediately obedient, but there are other truths revealed as we study more closely:

Truth #1: *A true servant is placed in charge of much (Gen. 24:2).*

Eliezer did not suddenly arrive at this much responsibility. God will give us more responsibility as we are faithful with a little of it (Matthew 25:21).

Truth #2: *A true servant asks questions to understand (Gen. 24:5).*

This is not a bad thing. Eliezer thought about possible outcomes and inquired as to what his response should be before he moved ahead. Assurance and confidence before the Lord is something we all need.

Truth #3: *A true servant is faithful (Gen. 24:9).*

Eliezer was not afraid to swear an oath. He was determined and consistent in his obedience. So, putting himself "out there" for risk under oath was something he took very seriously.

Truth #4: *A true servant shares the good things of the master (Gen. 24:10 and 53).*

We have a New Testament parallel. We serve in this walk and give to others from what we have been given. We love and bless others because God first loved us. He also has given us every spiritual blessing in Christ. Luke was inspired to pen, "Give, and you will receive. Your gift will return to you in full – pressed down, shaken together to make room for more, running over and poured into your lap. The amount you give will determine the amount you get back (Luke 6:38 NLT)."

Truth #5: *A true servant prays for those being served (Gen. 24:12).*

A whole-hearted servant maintains focus on those he or she is serving. At some point, I began to pray more boldly about my study time. Before, my prayer had been, "Teach *me*, Lord, and that will be enough." Now I pray, "If this is a good work, Lord, teach and bless others through it. Allow it to bear much fruit according to your will (Col. 1:10)." I do not ask this in a self-serving way. I pray God will reveal great things to you by the power of His Word. Who are you serving? Pray now for those you are serving, in whatever capacity, that the Lord would minister in ways they can clearly know His ministering Spirit.

Truth #6: *A true servant knows the favor of the Lord (Gen. 24:15).*

Rebekah appeared as the chosen wife for Isaac before Eliezer had even finished his prayer! Additionally, the servant was given a place to stay and Rebekah was turned over to him as the Lord's favor was noticeable by even Rebekah's family (vs. 31 and 50).

So many times, we want God's favor, but don't feel worthy of it. We are not worthy of His favor, except by the blood of the Lamb. But when we are in Christ, we can expect it as true servants, even in the midst of heartache and suffering. We can know His favor in the best or worst of times. Our circumstances are not indicators of whether or not we have it. Your heart knows when He has placed His favor there.

Truth #7: *A true servant gives all the glory to God (Gen. 24:26 and 52).*

A worker for the Lord might attempt to share glory as we saw in the story of Jehu. Eliezer wanted those present and his God to know that he bowed in sacrifice of praise for what his God had done. You and I must realize that God cannot fully use us if we want to share glory with Him.

Truth #8: *A true servant is unwavering in obedience (Gen. 24:56).*

Eliezer met with compromise after everything had been settled, or so he thought. It seems Rebekah's mother began to realize that this good thing for her daughter would actually cause her own heart to ache. Even so, Eliezer and Rebekah whole-heartedly submitted to what the Lord had orchestrated. What has the Lord asked you to do recently that you obeyed without wavering? Listen for His voice. Trust and obey. Obedience is easier each time, especially when we entrust the outcome to God.

A Servant's "Be" Attitudes

And we, who with unveiled faces all reflect the Lord's glory, are being transformed into his likeness with ever-increasing glory, which comes from the Lord, who is spirit.
II Cor. 3:18 NIV

    The chief servant of Abraham is an example of many faithful ones in the Old Testament. Now, we'll search for the look of a true servant for us as New Testament believers, with the addition of one more Old Testament reference.

    I read an article recently about one of those "mega" banks. The bank's research revealed its predecessors had owned slaves prior to the Civil War. The bank issued apologies in the media and also committed funding toward black history education. We, however, don't want to make apologies for our service to Christ when He returns.

    Fortunately, slavery has been abolished here in America – and years ago. However, service is still our calling in Christ. We bow down in submission to our Master. First we are called servants, and then we are called friends. These scriptures outline the requirements of the servant. Think of them as a **Servant's "Be" Attitudes:**

Jeremiah 46:27-28	Be not afraid.
Matthew 8:9	Be submissive.
Matthew 10:24	Be humble.
Luke 12:4-7	Be fearful of God alone.
Luke 16:13	Be devoted wholly to one Master.
Ephesians 6:5-6	Be obedient to God's will.
II Timothy 2:24	Be kind, teaching others.

Of these "Be" Attitudes, which ones would you consider "done deals" toward the Lord and others? Which ones are still being compromised in your walk?

Pray now asking the Lord to help you in the "Be" Attitudes you have not whole-heartedly obeyed. Thank Him for the ones that are settled in your life. I'm grateful the Lord allows us to see progress in a few things. As we give Him rule in our hearts, we'll find there is another teachable moment just around the corner. As II Corinthians 3:18 (see page 112) motivates, each teachable moment is another opportunity to become more like Christ.

Years ago, my oldest child asked me something he'd never asked before: "Mom, do people get paid to work for the Lord?" The answer is difficult to put in words that an 11-year old can understand. "Yes, in a thousand ways." I went on to tell him what scripture says: every good work we do to the glory of the Lord lays up treasures in heaven where nothing can destroy them. "Son, many who work for the Lord also get paid in different ways right here on earth." For me, one of the most awesome rewards is to see someone begin to devour God's Word like a good steak and potato dinner. More than any payment or other benefit, I want to hear the Lord say, "Well done, thou good and faithful servant. You have been faithful with a few things; I will put you in charge of many things. Come and share your master's happiness." (Matthew 25:21 *KJV*)

Servant-Leader, Jesus

Your attitude should be the same as that of Christ Jesus: Who, being in very nature God, did not consider equality with God something to be grasped, but made himself nothing, taking the very nature of a servant, being made in human likeness. Phil. 2:5-7 NIV

Since we must first be servants before the Lord considers us friends, one more question deserves an answer. Knowing Christ as the ultimate and perfect servant of God, what can we learn from His ministry? Just as the Lord has asked me, I'm asking you to pay particular attention to common threads throughout this book.

Before we end, we'll inspect the commonalities as we weave the final threads together. Equally as important, zoom in on things you've never seen in quite the same way before now. The Lord has a way of using a passage you've known all your life to reveal something different. What happens, then, is the truth revealed will melt into your heart making it difficult to ever forget. Praise you, Lord!

There has never been a servant like Christ, nor will there ever be. Surely, we'll see some things that are very different and moving in His life as He bowed to the will of His Father. I knew we'd eventually get to Him, and I'm so glad we have. Taking a long look at Jesus is always challenging. John said there wouldn't be enough room even in the whole world to record everything Christ did during His short three years of ministry (John 21:25). But there *is* so much recorded! Another reason it's difficult is because we see ourselves lacking every time we look at Him. Oh, the joy of knowing there will come a day when we'll be able to look at Him face-to-face and be like Him (I John 3:2).

Until then, each time we look at this Servant and wish for days we are more like Him, be encouraged. We may not be like Him until we see Him as He is. But, we can be *more* like Him. It's our charge as growing Christians and true servants (II Corinthians 3:18).

The Suffering Servant

An account of prophecy foretold by Isaiah regards Jesus as the Suffering Servant long before Mary ever knew

He was on the way. In Isaiah 52 and 53, we find at least three references about the degree of suffering this Servant would face: He would be rejected by men, stricken by God, and His life poured out unto death.

    The attempt at a horrific and realistic depiction of Christ's suffering was seen by millions in *The Passion of the Christ.* The real event was far worse. If it had been an exact depiction, we would not have recognized Jesus as a human being when they took His body from the cross (Isaiah 52:14). My sister went to see the movie before I did. When I asked her about it, she pointed out this very obvious difference. The film was kinder than the real thing. His crucifixion really happened. Our sin caused His extreme suffering, a brutality that no one will experience in the same way - at least no one who is perfect. Will you take time now to review Isaiah 52:13 to Isaiah 53:12? This time, you'll see three positive outcomes from all the suffering that occurred: 1) by His wounds, we are healed, 2) His punishment brought us peace, and 3) the will of the Lord will prosper in His hands.

    The saved and unsaved alike suffer, though Christ endured far more than we will ever face. Our Creator planned the sequence of events. He allowed His own Son to suffer in life and death the way He did. One reason is so we would know that Christ understands what suffering is and can identify with us when we suffer. The more we share in Christ's suffering, the more we will know Him (Phil. 3:10). Christ took on the very nature of a servant, then He was exalted. One day every knee will bow to him; every tongue confess that He is Lord (Phil. 2:5-11).

    We shy away from pain and suffering. In fact, I'll admit going to great lengths to avoid it at all cost for as long as possible. We may even convince ourselves that the absence of it is the goal of life. The last passage we'll review gives us hope in the midst of suffering. It will be an encouraging place to end.

When we suffer for the sake of Christ, we are in good company. As Matthew 5:10 tells us, we will see the kingdom of heaven. It's exactly what Stephen saw the day of his stoning (see Acts 7:54-60). Lord, move our hearts to accept suffering for your sake with joy knowing that we will see the kingdom of heaven.

Jesus, Ministering and Obedient

Jesus went throughout Galilee, teaching in their synagogues, preaching the good news of the kingdom, and healing every disease and sickness among the people.
Matt. 4:23 NIV

We move ahead to more characteristics of Christ as the perfect example of a Servant. We want to learn as much about how to be a true servant of Christ as we do about what it takes to be called His friend. It all starts with serving. We bow to that truth and continue to pull in more knowledge and wisdom. Sincere time doing in-depth Bible study will not leave you unchanged. It can't, because there is so much accomplishing power in every word. It will not return void (Isaiah 55:11), so keep pressing on for more knowledge, wisdom, and depth of insight.

The Ministering Servant

Matthew 4:23 records three acts of ministry Jesus did and is still doing today: teaching, preaching, and healing. We are also made ministers. This responsibility of servanthood is not left up to the preachers, prophets, and Jesus alone. Many places in scripture point to all believers as ministers, so don't immediately think this job is not for you. We can minister in many ways that do not involve preaching and prophecy. For one reference, look at

II Corinthians 3:6 where we are described as competent ministers.

To see the context of II Cor. 3:6, look back at verses 4 and 5. Our confidence is through Christ, and our competence is from God. Otherwise, I'd be an insecure mess, wouldn't you? This verse takes away any excuse we might conjure not to minister. But if we place our confidence in any other thing (our own abilities or resources, our church, or another person), we risk being boastful and vulnerable. We have full permission to boast in this: He who began a good work in me will be faithful to complete it (Phil. 1:6).

To prove our position as one of ministry, we can follow the example of Christ who came not to be served, but to serve (Matt. 20:28).

The Obedient Servant

There's that word again – obedience. Obedience, when all you heard was a gentle whisper. Obedience, when it deals with the smallest details of your day and the biggest decisions of your life. It's easier said than done. For Christ, it was no different. He was all man and all God. All man meant He had a free will, a choice, just like we do. All God meant He was about His Father's business, first and foremost. But He was not a robot! I have questions I want to ask when I see Him face-to-face. We'll have all the time in the world. I'll eventually get to ask my questions like, "Why did you cry at Lazarus' tomb? Why did you wait until Jarius' daughter was dead? Why did you sweat like drops of blood in the garden? Was obedience to your Father, at times, difficult for you too? Did you sometimes want to act sooner to avoid the heartache of your closest friends or the grieving parents of a dead daughter? Was your agony in the garden so great because you knew (and were already feeling) the pain obedience would cause you?" I'm not sure getting answers will matter as much there as it does here. Let's look at Christ's relationship with His Father where it concerns obedience:

- Jesus never spoke out of turn. (Matt. 20:23)
- Jesus' entire purpose on earth was to do the will of His Father. (Hebrews 10:5-7)
- Jesus only does what He sees His Father doing. (John 5:19)
- Jesus gave up His own will to pursue His Father's will. (Mark 14:35-36)
- Jesus obeyed so that God would be glorified and men would be drawn to God through Him. (John 12:27-28)

Remember Jesus washing the feet of His disciples? He was a servant not only to His Father, but also to men. I had a unique opportunity to hear renowned pastor and author David Jeremiah speak recently. His closing remark is one I will not soon forget. "We serve God by serving others."[23] He went on to say (and I paraphrase) that there's no way around it. If we think serving God is some lofty responsibility elevating us above everyday people, places and opportunities, we are mistaken.

Servants act for the good of others and for the glory of God.

Servanthood has been and always will be about people and relationships because God is about people and relationships.

Who We Serve

And being found in appearance as a man, he humbled himself and became obedient to death – even death on a cross! Therefore God exalted him to the highest place and gave him the name that is above every name that at the name of Jesus every knee should bow, in heaven and on earth and under the earth, and every tongue confess that Jesus Christ is Lord, to the glory of God the Father.
Philippians 2:8-11NIV

Christ was called a Servant in the early prophecies of Isaiah (Isaiah 42:1). And we are also called to be servants. In John 12:26, a two-part message is meant for you and me. The Command: Whoever serves me must follow me. The Encouragement: My Father will honor the one who serves me.

God will place servants where He is at work.

I'm clinging to one special promise as I serve the Lord Jesus and others. I can't imagine it, but God's Word says it's true. Jesus tells what *will* take place when we who have served Him get to see Him. I sang a song all my life that finds some of its basis in the truth of Luke 12:37, but I never really knew what it meant. I never paid attention that closely. I sang those old hymns every week at church. Now, they bring me to tears. I can almost hear the chords of this one: *Brethren, We Have Met to Worship.*

In Luke 12:37, we are told that Christ will dress himself to serve, and have those who have served Him recline at the table, and He will wait on them. As the song comes to a close, the verse sounds sweet to my ears:

Let us love our God supremely,
Let us love each other too;

> *Let us love and pray for sinners,*
> *Till our God makes all things new.*
> *Then He'll call us home to heaven,*
> *At His table we'll sit down;*
> *Christ will gird Himself, and serve us*
> *With sweet manna all around.*[24]

That's something to anticipate with joy! We have one more angle to review regarding servanthood. The Apostle Paul didn't have opportunity to walk with Christ in the flesh, and neither did we. He did, however, cross paths with at least some of the original twelve disciples. He learned in unique ways that we are only afforded through his inspired writings. What does he tell us? What can we learn from him about serving the Lord and others? We'll highlight some of his teachings regarding servanthood.

Mind of Christ

Some people think alike. Jackie is my precious friend. She is younger, and she never lets me forget it! I know we'll be friends when I'm 80 and she's in her 70s. I have a feeling she'll still be reminding me of her youthfulness. Many times, people ask, "Are you two sisters?" No, we're not even blood relatives. Our husbands are the ones that are related. Though they grew up together, Jackie and I were placed together when she married Scott. Even my sister has mistaken her for me on the phone! We resemble each other in many ways. Years ago, we ordered backpacks for our kids online. Anyone looking over our shoulders would have enjoyed the show. We were barely communicating by most standards, but all the sighs, unfinished sentences and facial expressions were enough for us. We accomplished the goal, and the backpacks arrived. First Corinthians 2:16 tells us that we are to have the mind of Christ. And it is His Spirit that works in us to act according to His purposes (Phil. 2:12-13).

The more we grow in Christ, the more He will grow in us! We will begin to have the mind of Christ. It's endearing to know the Lord placed Jackie and me together. She's such a blessing. We don't try to think alike or work hard at having similar mannerisms. We do, however, want to have the mind of Christ. The more time we spend with the Lord, the more blessing He'll be to us, and others will closely relate us to Him. We can have the mind of Christ.

Contentment in Christ

Contentment is one of the most difficult disciplines for us who live in America, the land of the free. I'm blessed to live here, and there is no other place I'd rather be. Visit, yes. Live, no. I've had opportunity to visit other countries, but only on vacation. So far, I've not had the rare chance to experience living conditions of an impoverished people. Our choices are endless, while the impoverished would not know how to handle choices at all. Even if cash isn't available for what we want or need to live comfortably, many can still acquire *it* on credit. What we acquire will not make us content. The Apostle Paul chose contentment and encourages us to do the same as Christ's servants and friends.

To us as believers, some passages stand out as landmarks on the roadmap of life. The Lord used Gal. 1:10 to open my eyes to the question, 'Who are you serving?' When we are trying to please men, we cannot possibly be a servant of Christ. It hit home. I pray He will use it in your life, if He hasn't already. What is your present state of mind? Are you a servant of men in trying to please them, or a servant of Christ in trying to please Him? On this point, we must choose.

I wanted the approval of my husband and the love and pleasure of my children, the affirmation of my church family, and church leadership. I have wished for the support and encouragement of my in-laws, as well as my boss. I so hoped, and still do, that anyone with whom I cross paths will respect and appreciate me. It's important to me, and always will be. But the Lord is transforming my "people-pleaser" heart. If in serving Him, I win the favor of man, fine. My call and desire is to please my Lord and Savior Jesus Christ. My contentment is in Christ. Whether or not you realize it, your contentment is also in Christ. No person or thing you serve will serve you in return quite enough to make you happy or content. Only Christ can do that. In fact, Scripture tells us an awesome truth about Christ as he grew in Luke 2:52. He gained wisdom/stature, and favor with both God and man. As we grow in our relationship with the Lord, we will no longer seek the favor of men, though we may likely receive it as we also please the Lord.

What a lesson I've learned from His voice to me in Galatians 1:10! I've found no greater contentment than that of knowing the Lord, His blessing, and favor. Let's review the words of a song that resonate with my new heart. The Lord has helped me look up and give Him glory. May the words of this song be a blessing and charge to you as you seek to serve the Lord and please Him alone:

Legacy

I don't mind if you've got something nice to say about me
And I enjoy an accolade like the rest
And you could take my picture and hang it in a gallery
Of all the Who's Who's and So-and-So's
That used to be the best at such and such
It wouldn't matter much

I won't lie, it feels alright to see your name in lights
We all need an "Atta Boy" or "Atta Girl"
But in the end I'd like to hang my hat on more besides
The temporary trappings of this world.

I want to leave a legacy
How will they remember me?
Did I choose to love?
Did I point to you enough
To make a mark on things?
I want to leave an offering
A Child of mercy and grace
Who blessed your name unapologetically
And leave that kind of legacy

Don't have to look too far or too long awhile
To make a lengthy list of all that I enjoy
It's an accumulating trinket and a treasure pile
That moth and rust, thieves and such will soon
Enough destroy.

Not well-traveled, not well-read
Not well-to-do, or well-bred
Just want to hear instead
Well done, good and faithful one

I don't mind if you've got something
nice to say about me[18]

Heir with Christ

I love "oh, by the way" benefits. It seems everywhere we've turned in scripture, "oh, by the way" blessings of servitude surface. Galatians 4:1-7 is no different. We are encouraged that though we are called servants, we are also called heirs. According to this passage, several benefits of being heirs with Christ are evident: we own the whole estate; we are redeemed; we have the full rights of sons; the Spirit of God's own Son resides in our hearts; God is our Abba Father; and we are heirs to His kingdom.

Many times in the New Testament, the apostles referred to themselves as servants of Christ, and gladly so. II Peter 1:1a is an example: "Simon Peter, a servant and apostle of Jesus Christ,…"

We can understand why they would gladly be servants by way of our study. When we hold the position of servant, but are also called friends, and even heirs of the Father with Christ, we shouldn't mind serving. It's a humble place to be, and I have no problem bowing there.

We recently re-visited the Biltmore Mansion in Asheville, North Carolina. One reality dawned this time that I'd not noticed before: the servants' quarters. As we walked through room after room on three floors of beautifully embellished furnishings, something occurred to me. Though slavery is now abolished, I considered the wealth of Mr. Vanderbilt. After seeing the servants' quarters, I wouldn't have minded serving this wealthy master. Surely, they did not miss a meal. They had all they needed. Their living quarters may not have equaled the master's, but they had plenty because they were serving a master with plenty. Perhaps the leftovers would have been better than the meals I serve on most nights.

Our Father owns cattle on a thousand hills. One day, we'll walk the streets of purest gold and touch walls of jasper. The Word makes its dwelling in us richly. We have need of nothing that our Father in heaven does not know we need before we ask. I will serve Him with gladness and enter His courts with praise. The Mighty Master has done great things for me, His servant! To know I am an heir with Christ is hardly fathomable, yet true.

The position of servant is the only one I prefer with the Lord. In great mercy, He accepts us just as we are, but I'm glad He has so transformed me that I long to serve

Him. I bow down to this place, how about you? Pray to the Master of your life and ask Him to help you in being the servant, friend, and child He wants you to be. As we have tied a bow on what it means to be a servant, we will take a look at what it means to be a friend of Christ.

9
Now I Call You Friend

Perhaps by now you know that Christ has called you to befriend Him, as surely as you realize He has been your friend all along. We've taken some side roads on this journey that have been like field trips and learning experiences to determine what it means to be a friend of God. The invitation to befriend Christ was the first stop for me. Though I may be just pulling into a rest stop, I know the ride is not over. I hope we have many more miles to travel before He calls each of us home. I want Him to call me friend. What about you?

When we invest our most valuable commodity of time into going through a Bible study, listening to a sermon or Sunday school lesson, or participating in any similar activity, we should always ask, "So, what? What is the 'take home' value? How can what I've learned be a catalyst for change in my behavior? My life?"

We hope to answer these questions as our final destination. We'll arrive at the purpose of this book together by looking back over our shoulder with a good set of binoculars. Now that we've come to the end of this road, it's the best way to see where we've been. The vital question is this:

Can Christ confide in me?

"Where were you when I laid the earth's foundation?
Tell me, if you understand."
Job 38:4 NIV

Can He trust me with His plans and purposes, not only for my life, but for my family, church, community, and His world?

We come to our focal verses by way of a story or two. One of my children was in some kind of mood on a particular day years ago (name withheld to protect the innocent). It had been a busy weekend, and the kids played longer and harder than usual. On Sunday, "moody" practically woke up complaining. By the time he was dressed for church, his shirt collar was the issue. He liked the shirt, but not the collar. Then, his underwear was twisted. As we arrived at church, he noticed a clump of hair out of place. The day wore on, and he continued to complain. We've all had days like this. His daddy told him he was "hunting something to complain about." On the way to the evening service, he finally found it. Tucked away in the recesses of his mind was a time he had never forgotten. And he'd not forgiven those of us who were, to him, guilty.

He had recently been invited to several parties. Some conflicted with other events our family wanted to attend, which meant he would have to leave early from his parties. Here it is, end of summer. Months had passed, and he had found the most justifiable excuse for complaining that day.

I hate to leave a party early too. One day, I was begrudging something with the Lord. My heart had held it too long, so I had to unload. Like my child, I was having a pity-party anyway, so I may as well pick something for which to be pitiful. We are to approach the throne of grace with confidence that we may receive mercy and find grace to help in time of need. (Hebrews 4:16.) I often use my commute to work to do just that and to worship the Lord.

On this morning nearly a decade ago, the cork blew on my bottle and the tearful words began to flow: "Lord, why do some women say their husbands are their best friends? Why can't I say the same thing? I love him dearly. He's a wonderful husband and a loving, compassionate father. But I don't have that kind of relationship with him. I can't honestly say that he is my best friend. I know it takes years to arrive at that, but we've got those years, Lord! I can often share my heart more easily with my closest girlfriends. It makes me so mad! Why, Lord?"

After I poured out my heart to Him, a quiet hush came over me. I didn't want to listen to my usual praise songs. I could almost feel the sag in my face as my muscles gravitated to the lowest point. My bottom lip was in danger of being stuck between my foot and the gas pedal that day. I said all I knew to say. Then, He responded with a question. Can you think of a time God questioned you in response to your question? How does God respond when you have a pity-party right at His feet?

You are in good company if you've been questioned by God. If you will, take time to read Job 38 now. You'll see that Job had many questions, and the Lord finally responds in this chapter and the three that follow it.

The Lord approached me in a way I was not expecting. Sometimes we just want Him to fix our problems. Why should I expect to come home and discover that my husband had been "blinded by the light" and sees me in a new way, as his best friend? Or, that I would suddenly see him as mine? Most issues like this do not change overnight, though we somehow expect them to (but we'd never admit it). God can fix it overnight, but He usually doesn't. There is often a greater purpose in long-term transformation. His response to me that morning was in the form of a question. "If Gary was your best friend, what would that make me?" I'll share more about my response later to such a bold question from the Lord straight to my heart. For now, consider who your friends are, and what supporting roles they play in your life. Christ is the Best Friend of all friends. Give Him a chance to be yours today.

When the Lord speaks to our hearts in a gentle and bold way, we are wise to respond. I humbly responded to His question with more tears. "Is that really what you said, Lord?" I felt His graceful embrace. I prayed, "Lord, I'll never complain about this again. It's forever settled. Thank You, Lord!"

Yes, it is settled. I am grateful that my Savior and Lord is also my best Friend. You can't top that in any mate, parent, or other important relationship in your life. No matter how close you are to someone, there is no comparison to the intimacy that can be attained in a relationship with Christ. But, it's something we must seek with Him, just as we do with a spouse or a close friend. Intimacy in relationship doesn't happen without investment. God has invested His Son, the perfect sacrifice, the spotless Lamb, that we might know and fellowship with Him. He calls us the bride of Christ. If that is not a portrait of ultimate intimacy, I'm not sure what is. How would you describe your relationship with the Lord right now?

God will respond to our queries, sometimes in a statement and other times with a question. Or you may sense no response at all. It will be worth the wait if you have yet to hear Him speak concerning a matter you've committed to prayer. I had bottled and corked the concern of friendship with my mate for years. For the first time, my concern made it to God in the form of a prayer. Do you have a concern that you begrudge and complain about in your thoughts and attitudes, but never utter in prayer? If so, will you commit it to prayer today?

Interestingly enough, the Lord settled the question of friendship in my heart months before He asked me to befriend Him. The question, the burden of my heart, and His response all line up with His purposes. We don't always get to look back and see that, but other times it's as clear as a mountain lake on a crisp winter morning. To know His purposes, we must seek Him as deliberately and instinctively as a newborn seeks the breast of his mother. (Jeremiah 29:11-13)

If the Lord had not already settled this issue with me, how could I have understood Him calling me to be *His* friend? Will you answer the call? Will you be a friend of the Lord? Over these last few pages, we'll weave the realities of friendship together as we depend on our best Friend to guide us.

We Bow Down

But he gives us more grace. That is why Scripture says, "God opposes the proud but gives grace to the humble."
James 4:6 NIV

We still have a few scriptures to stitch into this book. Each of them twist together for a strong, yet common thread that will not be a surprise to you. The words of John 15:13 tell us of no greater love than the love of a friend who will lay down his life for you. I think first of Christ as the One who lays down His life, but what about you and me? Are you willing to lay down your life for your Friend, Christ? Most of us will not be called to martyrdom for Christ in the sense of giving up our physical body to death for His cause. But what about things we count profitable and hold to so tightly? If they keep us from truly serving and becoming a friend of Christ, what are we to do with them? Paul counted them as worthless (Philippians 3:7-8), as garbage so that he could gain Christ and become one with Him.

We are called to lay down our lives and anything in them we consider profitable. I have a dear friend who, like most women, counts profitable the things that make her a woman: her breasts, her figure, her beautiful hair. Right now, she is giving those things up, one by one. With breast cancer and the various treatments, she had said good-bye to her hair for a season. She has had a double mastectomy and more treatment. Kathy is a real trooper. She realizes God is in control, though she battles her flesh every day as she lays down her very life before Him. She's a beautiful woman with a wonderful husband and three precious boys.

She may lose a lot, but she will never lose her womanhood. After all, she's the only one in her household! God created her to be a woman after His heart, first and foremost. He knows the way she takes, her sacrifice, and what is being gained for His glory. We are also called to lay down our life for our Friend.

The best kept secrets always have a way of getting out. If you are a friend of God, you will not have to tell a soul. Your life will testify of your relationship with the Creator. Your God will reveal it. And you will be humbled by it. In Luke 14:7-10, there is a story about humility. A guest who enters a wedding feast should be careful where he sits for there may be another person who is more distinguished or highly regarded by the host, and that person may be asked to sit in that place. So, we are best to sit in a place of humility. If the host wishes to have you or me at a more distinguished position, he will tell us – "Friend, we have a better place for you!" (v. 10).

Scripture reveals that we are enemies of God if we are friends of the world (James 4:4-10). Our key word "friendship" glares in the first sentence of this passage. Immediately, James offers a prescription for a cure – humble yourself before God. That's what I need, don't you? An illness without a cure brings a terrible prognosis. The cure itself can be a costly investment, but well worth it in the end.

The position of friendship is a humble place to be according to the Scriptures. That's the first common thread. Several more will knit this work together in a meaningful way.

Though the position of friendship is one of humility, it is a very close place to be. Are you a friend to Christ who sticks closer than a brother? What is the reality of friendship with Christ in your own life? If this book had been about what others are to us, or what we are looking for in a friend, it would not have been what God asked me to put into writing. Certainly, many of the concepts and exhortations we've journeyed through over the last few chapters and pages, when fully engaged, would make us better friends, spouses, parents, co-workers, and any other position you might hold in life. However, the primary focus is this: Can Christ confide in you? Can He call you His friend?

When we befriend God, we will supernaturally be in right relationship with those around us. I pray as you complete this book, you'll understand the places in the path of friendship with your Lord that need smoothing out, and the places you freely travel. Ask the Lord to walk with you in intimate friendship. In what ways can we stick to Christ closer than a brother?

This review of our study may be more meaningful for me than for you because it's something I love to do. When I pen a letter, I review it. I fold the letter, place it in the envelope only to flip it open, take the letter out, and read it as if I have received it. Repetition in the form of review is a good thing. The common threads deserve a final weave together, and into our hearts. But first, I'd like to ask you a question. Of all that you've read on friendship with Christ, what has the Lord illuminated most to your heart?

Ask the Lord to plunge these illuminated truths deep into your heart now so that His commands *to* you become part *of* you as you walk with Him. Ask Him to forever change you as it concerns what only His Spirit could reveal. We've already hit on one reality of friendship:

Being a friend of Christ is a position of humility.

Now, we'll see more common threads of friendship. And we bow to Him as humbly as our human hearts can to be called friends of God.

The Weave of Friendship

"You are my friends if you do what I command."
John 15:14 NIV

Let's look at the commonalities of this work on friendship with God as a weave of sorts. It is the woven thread that makes the fabric. In the life of a Christian, the weave has its basis in our relationship to Christ. The fabric of our life is the result of the weave. The quality of the weave always determines the strength and beauty of the fabric, both figuratively and literally.

Being a friend of Christ requires obedience.

You will notice obedience as an element of friendship with God, whether we were looking at Peter and the other disciples, Abraham, Moses, or servants of God. Obedience requires risk, I know. It also requires faith and trust in the One you serve. Not only does acting with obedience take faith, it also has a unique way of building faith. Every time we obey the whispered command, the next time is easier. The tasks, however, often increase in difficulty. Haven't you noticed this? The more you give God, the more He is able to require of your life. Lay it down. Trust and obey. As we mention trust, another element of friendship with Christ presents itself:

Being a friend of Christ depends on your response to His invitation.

If you have not already trusted Christ, committed your life to Him and accepted His invitation to eternal life, what better time than now to do it? If you have not made such a life changing decision, this will reveal the simplicity and faith of such a move.

Don't keep the faith! Pass it on! I had been a Christian since I was a child, but it wasn't until my 30s that I was able to lead someone to Christ. He orchestrated a fun summer visit from my niece that would turn out to be so much more. I had no idea what He had planned, but it was an awesome (and treacherous) opportunity for me to lead her to a personal relationship with Him.

It takes a child-like faith, and I pray that my own children are even now being equipped to lead others to Christ. The resource we used in our home many years to do nightly devotions with our children has a wonderful, simple way of explaining the steps of faith. The Christian life is described as an adventure, and that it is. Next, I will invite you to walk through these steps of faith and pray to the best Friend you will ever have to blaze the trail of adventure with you. If today is the day to take those steps, then don't wait. Talk to a pastor or trusted Christian friend that can lead you through the steps that will bring life as you've never experienced before.

I can't imagine a privilege more rewarding than having the opportunity to lead someone to Christ. If you are that someone, thank you so much for allowing me to walk through this with you. The journey with your Creator is an amazing one. Here are the three steps of faith, simple enough for even a small child to understand:

A – Admit
Admit to God that you are a sinner. A sinner is someone who has disobeyed God's rules. The Bible says that everyone has disobeyed God. Tell God you want to stop sinning and start believing in Him. (Romans 3:23; Romans 6:23; Acts 3:19; I John 1:9)

B – Believe
Believe that Jesus is God's only Son who died on the cross for your sins. When Jesus died and was raised from the dead, He took the blame for your sins. Because of what Jesus did, God will forgive your sins if you ask Him. (John 3:16; John 14:6; Romans 5:8)

C – Confess
Confess or tell others about your faith in Jesus. Tell them how Jesus died for you. Tell them you want to follow His commands and His example of loving God and loving others. Tell your pastor, your Sunday school teacher, and your parents. Your pastor can help you tell the people in your church that you began the adventure of becoming a Christian. Get involved in a Bible believing church. (Romans 10:9-10; 13) [25]

Now, as you continue to respond to Christ's call on your life, consider some final elements of friendship.

Being a friend of Christ requires reverent fear and worship of Him.

Friendship with Christ should be ever before us as we seek to serve Him. I'm afraid, however, that it has little relevance to many Christians. We can often live in such a way that we do not fear the God we serve. Perhaps we do not fear Him because we do not truly know Him. We know Him, yes, but only as the God we learned about in Sunday school or growing up. The process of truly knowing God comes primarily through in-depth study of Scripture. We will have a healthy fear and compelling worship of God when we begin to truly know Him.

Being a friend of Christ allows Him to mold you into His image.

We are like potter's clay according to Scripture. How hard or soft is your clay? The fingers of God work with us as we allow Him. The potter sits perched on a stool, leaning into the blob on the wheel. He looks intently at the color, the texture. The clay must be pliable to mold into the beautiful vessel he has envisioned. The potter is patient as he reworks the clay, sometimes beginning again at the blob on the wheel.

Being a friend of Christ reveals God's glory in you and to others.

According to II Corinthians 3:18, once the veil of our unbelief is removed and we are believing Christians by the blood of Jesus, we will begin to reflect the glory of God. His Spirit will do its powerful work in making us more and more like Christ. And as we become more like Him, we are changed into His glorious image. Don't ask me how that happens, but I've seen it on faces and in lives since I was old enough to remember. I encourage you to turn this passage into a personal prayer today:

"Whoever serves me must follow me;
and where I am, my servant also will be.
My Father will honor the one who serves me."
John 12:26 NIV

As we continue to weave the last common threads of this work together, they are more about the exterior of our lives, or what others see. The degree to which we diligently weave the interior threads will determine how beautiful and strong the fabric of our life is to the world around us. There are several threads that impact the quality of the fabric that those around us see, hear, and feel from our lives. We've looked at them, but let's examine them one last time.

Being a friend of Christ demands willing service to Him and others.

Serving comes naturally to some, but not to others. If we are careful to keep pride in check, we will bow with gladness to serve. We will serve those who seem to have earned it and others we would desire to serve least. Our service in the Body of Christ and to those who are lost will only be effective when we are empowered by the Holy Spirit and have pure motives. There is no escaping our responsibility to serve. We surely do not want the rewards of serving to escape us.

Our scripture reminder for this truth is found in Philippians 2:5-11. We must have the same attitude Christ did. We are sons and daughters of the living God, but we do not proudly cling to such a thought. Instead, we give up our rights as royal heirs and serve. We humble ourselves before God and are obedient to His commands. We serve Christ by serving others. Today, remember that. Hold a door open for someone. Offer to do something unexpected to help one who needs it. You will not have to look far. God will show you exactly who that someone is. And that will be your moment of truth. Will you obey?

Being a friend of Christ frees Him to pour blessing and favor on you.

As Abraham's seed, we can claim God's covenant promise of blessing given to him years ago. Through Abraham's family, Jesus Christ was born to save us. And in Christ, we have wonderful blessing and favor through His sacrificial blood of atonement. Though it is far more than we deserve, His covenant promise to Abraham is still ours.

Confiding Secrets

The Lord confides in those who fear him;
He makes his covenant known to them.
Psalm 25:14 NIV

In *My Utmost for His Highest,* Oswald Chambers discloses what makes my heart beat every day. It's what I live for everyday – to know the secrets of the Lord and to have Him confide in me and share with me. Now that I have an intimate relationship with Him, I only want to move up the mountain to higher planes. Chambers writes:

What is the sign of a friend? That he tells you secret sorrows? No, that he tells you secret joys. Many confide to you their secret sorrows, but the last mark of intimacy is to confide secret joys. Have we ever let God tell us any of His joys, or are we telling God our secrets so continually that we leave no room for Him to talk to us?[26]

He knows every detail of our individual lives. Sharing secret joys with the Lord is ultimate pleasure and fellowship. To know His will without asking and to have the mind of Christ without thinking about it, that is true unity with the Father – true friendship. Christ has confided His secret joys when:

- ❖ Your eyes flood with tears at a baptism service.
- ❖ You are overwhelmed with it as you see or show kindness to someone in need.
- ❖ Your heart swells as you notice a tiny step of progress in your walk with the Lord, or in the walk of another Christian.
- ❖ You worship Him and can't resist flinging your arms up in praise, too.
- ❖ You are obedient in the smallest request from Him; then, you know His blessing and favor have rested on you that day.
- ❖ A heartfelt prayer has been answered and faith has greatly increased in the lives of those involved.
- ❖ Someone finally comes around to the saving knowledge of Christ and makes a move toward Him.
- ❖ You feel the very arms of a loving God around you in the intimacy of your quiet time.

That, my friend, is really living in fellowship and friendship with Christ. Do we escape trouble? No. Just yesterday it knocked on my door. But, I know that as I rise each morning to bless the name of the Lord, again His mercy is fresh. His grace is present; my eyes are on Him. My burdens are lighter. I'd rather be with the Lord than anywhere else. He's my Friend. I'm His. What a privilege! What an honor! When have you been befriended by someone? What was your response?

Sociologists have a theory of the looking-glass self: You become what the most important person in your life (wife, father, boss, etc.) thinks you are. How would my life change if I truly believed the Bible's astounding words about God's love for me and if I looked in the mirror and saw what God sees?

Brennan Manning tells the story of an Irish priest who, on a walking tour of a rural parish, sees an old peasant kneeling by the side of the road, praying. Impressed, the priest says to the man, "You must be very close to God." The peasant looks up from his prayers, thinks a moment, and then smiles, "Yes, He's very fond of me."[27]

These days, friendship is harder to come by. The time needed to build friendships is even more difficult to find than the friends themselves. If you can remember a time when someone befriended you, then you know how it felt. The Lord desires your friendship. He's calling you. Listen. You will hear Him.

I come to the garden alone,
while the dew is still on the roses;
And the voice I hear, falling on my ear,
the Son of God discloses.
He speaks, and the sound of His voice
is so sweet the birds hush their singing;
And the melody that He gave to me,
within my heart is ringing.
I'd stay in the garden with Him
tho' the night around me be falling;
But He bids me go; thro' the voice of woe,
His voice to me is calling.
And He walks with me, and He talks with me,
and He tells me I am His own,
And the joy we share as we tarry there,
none other has ever known.[28]

He's very fond of you. Place Christ in that prominent position, the place of the most important person in your life, and become what He thinks you are. Be His friend just as He is yours.

It's been a privilege to serve you. It's been a blessing to open the pages of God's Word and see the mysterious love of the One who calls us His friends unveiled time after time. I treasure Him as a Friend. He treasures us as friends. May God's richest blessings be poured out upon your head. May you find in Christ – not just a better friend, but a best Friend. May He find in you His best friend too.

[1] Fannie Crosby, *The Baptist Hymnal* (Nashville, TN: Convention Press, 1991), 308.
[2] Darrell Evans, *Your Love is Extravagant*, Christian Lyrics Online.
[3] James Strong, from the *New Strong's Exhaustive Concordance of the Bible* (Nashville, TN: Thomas Nelson Publishers, 1996), 27.
[4] Application notes from the *Life Application® Bible,* New International Version® (Wheaton, IL: Tyndale House Publishers, Inc. and Grand Rapids, MI: Zondervan Publishing House, 1991), 1929.
[5] Strong, James, from the *New Strong's Exhaustive Concordance of the Bible,* (Nashville, TN: Thomas Nelson Publishers, 1996), 18.
[6] Ibid, 73.
[7] "Area Couple Aids in Establishing English-Speaking Church in Mendoza," *Mobile Register*, December. 17, 1960, 6-A.
[8] *DLEA Newsletter*, July 28, 2005, 1.
[9] James Strong, from the *New Strong's Exhaustive Concordance of the Bible* (Nashville, TN: Thomas Nelson Publishers, 1996), 83.
[10] James Strong, from the *New Strong's Exhaustive Concordance of the Bible* (Nashville, TN: Thomas Nelson Publishers, 1996), 133.
[11] Ibid, 3.
[12] Ibid, 8.
[13] Ibid, 96.
[14] Ibid, 43.
[15] Application notes from the *Life Application® Bible,* New International Version® (Wheaton, IL: Tyndale House Publishers and Grand Rapids, MI: Zondervan Publishing House, 1991), 2251.
[16] Rick Warren, *The Purpose Driven® Life* (Grand Rapids, MI: Zondervan, 2002), 275.
[17] *DLEA Newsletter*. October 1, 2004, 2.
[18] James Strong, from the *New Strong's Exhaustive Concordance of the Bible* (Nashville, TN: Thomas Nelson Publishers, 1991), 67.
[19] Ibid, 136.
[20] James Strong, from the *New Strong's Exhaustive Concordance of the Bible* (Nashville, TN: Thomas Nelson Publishers, 1996), 101.
[21] Ibid, 24-25.
[22] Application notes from the *Life Application® Bible,* New International Version® (Wheaton, IL: Tyndale House Publishers, Inc. and Grand Rapids, MI: Zondervan Publishing House, 1991), 625.
[23] David Jeremiah, from a message, Four Points Sheraton, Tuscaloosa, AL, Spring 2005.

[24] George Atkins, *The Baptist Hymnal* (Nashville, TN: Convention Press, 1991), 379.

[25] Nichole Nordeman, *Legacy* (Ariose Music/ASCAP/Admin. By EMI Christian Music/Sparrow Records, 2002).

[26] Oswald Chambers, *My Utmost for His Highest* (New York: Dodd, Mead & Company, 1963), 155.

[27] Philip Yancey, *What's So Amazing About Grace?* (Grand Rapids, MI: Zondervan Publishing House, 1997), 61.

[28] C. Austin Miles, *The Baptist Hymnal* (Nashville, TN: Convention Press, 1991), 187.

Copyright ©2006 by Mel Ann B. Sullivan
Copyright date: January 23, 2006
Copyright Registration Number: TXU1 – 282-199
ISBN-13: 978-1535374798
ISBN-10: 1535374799

All rights reserved.

No part of this work may be reproduced or transmitted in any form or by any means, electronic or mechanical, including photocopying and recording, or by any information storage or retrieval system, except as may be expressly permitted in writing by the author.

Requests for permission should be addressed in writing to Mel Ann Sullivan, 688 Beasley Road, Millry, AL 36558

Printed in the United States of America

Unless otherwise noted, Scripture quotations are from the Holy Bible, *New International Version*, copyright 1973, 1978, 1984 by International Bible Society. Used by permission of Zondervan Publishing House. All rights reserved.

The "NIV" and "New International Version" trademarks are registered in the United States Patent and Trademark Office by International Bible Society. Use of either trademark requires the permission of International Bible Society.

Cover image purchased through www.shutterstock.com. Back cover author portrait by Lorie Roach Photography. This book is also available in e-book and print at www.amazon.com.

Made in the USA
Charleston, SC
19 October 2016